RYA Day Skipper
for Motor Cruisers

by Jon Mendez

Illustrator: Pete Galvin

© Jon Mendez 2010
First Published 2010
The Royal Yachting Association
RYA House, Ensign Way, Hamble
Southampton SO31 4YA
Tel: 0844 556 9555
Fax: 0844 556 9516
E-mail: publications@rya.org.uk
Web: www.rya.org.uk
ISBN: 978-1906-435-554
RYA Order Code: G97

Totally Chlorine Free   Sustainable Forests

A CIP record of this book is available from the British Library.

Note: While all reasonable care had been taken in the preparation of this book, the publisher takes no responsibility for the use of the methods or products or contracts described in the book.

Illustrations and Cover Design: Pete Galvin

Typesetting and Design: Kevin Slater

Proofreading and indexing: Alan Thatcher

Printed in China through World Print

Contents

Some of the terms used throughout this book will be new to you. Explanations are given in the Glossary on page 88.

Introduction

More than 11,000 people, throughout the world, successfully complete a RYA Day Skipper Practical course every year.

The courses are run by RYA Training Centres around the UK and overseas. Using a RYA recognised centre will ensure that you are taught to the RYA's high standards, and your course will be safe, informative and enjoyable.

Day Skipper Handbook – Motor has been compiled to complement the Day Skipper Practical course and draws on the cumulative experience of hundreds of experienced instructors. The techniques shown or described are tried and tested and are suitable for most types of motorboat.

I hope that you enjoy the book and find it useful.

Good boating.

Richard Falk
RYA Chief Cruising Instructor

KEY TO SYMBOLS USED THROUGHOUT THE BOOK

 Engine ahead

 Engine neutral

 Engine astern

 Wind direction

 Intended route

 Stream/tide

 Transit

Parts of a motor cruiser

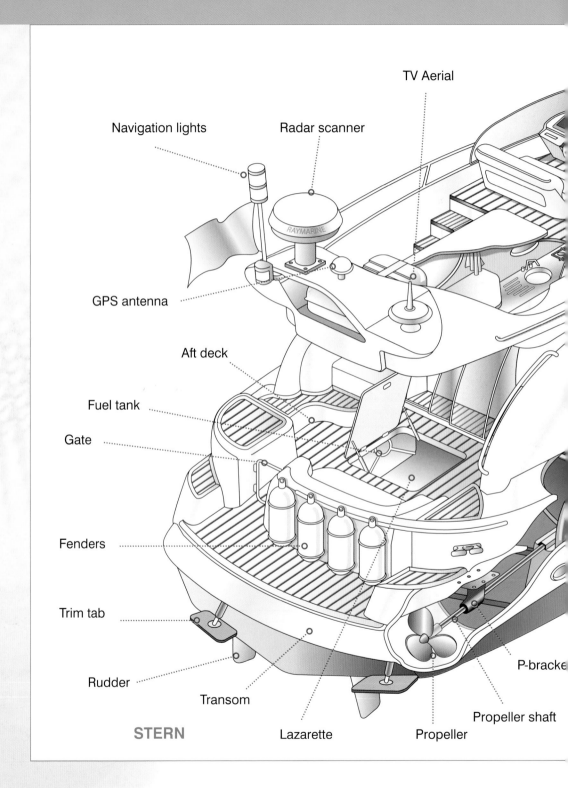

TV Aerial

Navigation lights

Radar scanner

GPS antenna

Aft deck

Fuel tank

Gate

Fenders

Trim tab

Rudder

Transom

STERN

Lazarette

Propeller

P-bracket

Propeller shaft

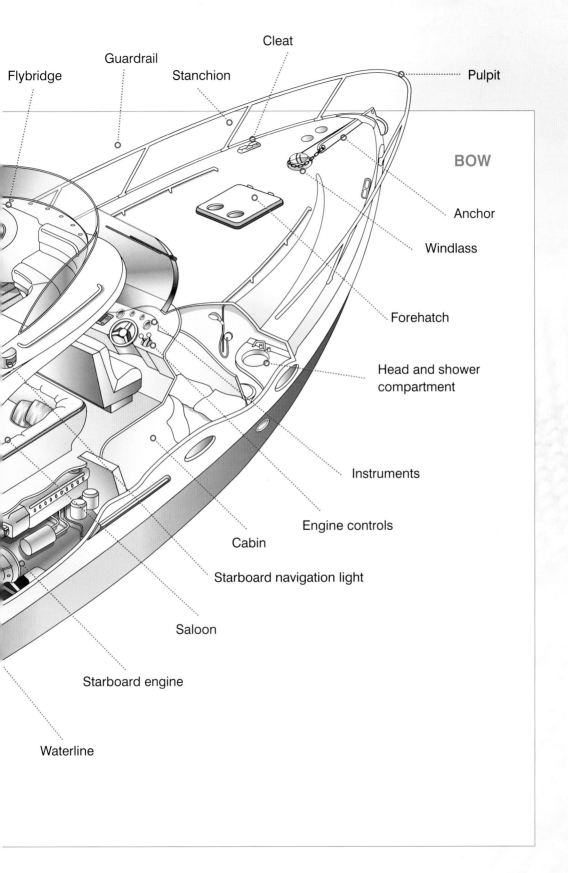

Cleat

Guardrail

Flybridge   Stanchion   Pulpit

BOW

Anchor

Windlass

Forehatch

Head and shower
compartment

Instruments

Engine controls

Cabin

Starboard navigation light

Saloon

Starboard engine

Waterline

Preparation for sea

Prepare the vessel for sea before leaving harbour. Brief the crew about the passage and consider the crew's strengths.

Crew
- Give a safety brief.
- Ensure they know the location and how to use all safety equipment.
- Brief the crew about the passage.
- Check if any crew have a medical condition you should be aware of.
- Check that all have lifejackets that are correctly adjusted. Carry harnesses for deck work.
- If any crew get sea sick, make sure they have taken medication.

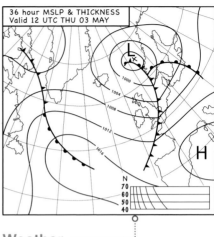

36 hour MSLP & THICKNESS
Valid 12 UTC THU 03 MAY

Weather
- Obtain a weather forecast; if on a longer passage, monitor the weather in the days leading up to the trip. If in a tidal area, find out tidal direction.

Fuel
- Check there is sufficient fuel.

FUEL

HIGHLY FLAMMABLE

25 LITRES

Victualling

■ Ensure there is enough food and drinks for the voyage.
■ Prepare food in advance as it is very difficult to cook en-route
on smaller motor boats.
■ Stow provisions in dry readily accessible places.

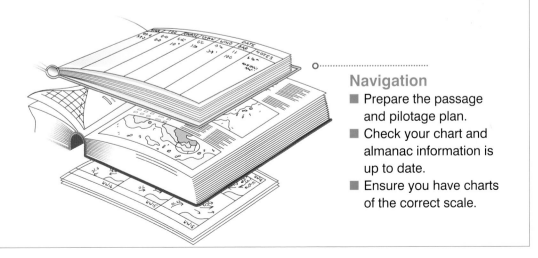

Navigation

■ Prepare the passage
and pilotage plan.
■ Check your chart and
almanac information is
up to date.
■ Ensure you have charts
of the correct scale.

Engine checks

Daily engine checks are the best way to ensure long engine life, reliability and to spot potential problems. Engine and fuel problems are one of the most common causes of callouts to rescue services and are preventable by regular checks and monitoring.

Daily checks

Daily – every day you use the boat, check the oil, water (fresh and seawater), fuel and belts for signs of wear and leaks.

Engine start procedure

All engines are different, however the same principles apply. Check batteries on. Ensure sea cocks are open, turn on ignition, start engines, monitor all gauges. If visible, check cooling water from exhausts.

Tools / Spares

Carry a tool kit and some basic spares, belts, impellor, oil and fuel filters and spare fluids.

DIPSTICK – check level is between marks, if discoloured or milky call an engineer

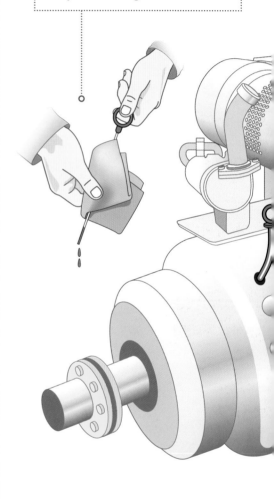

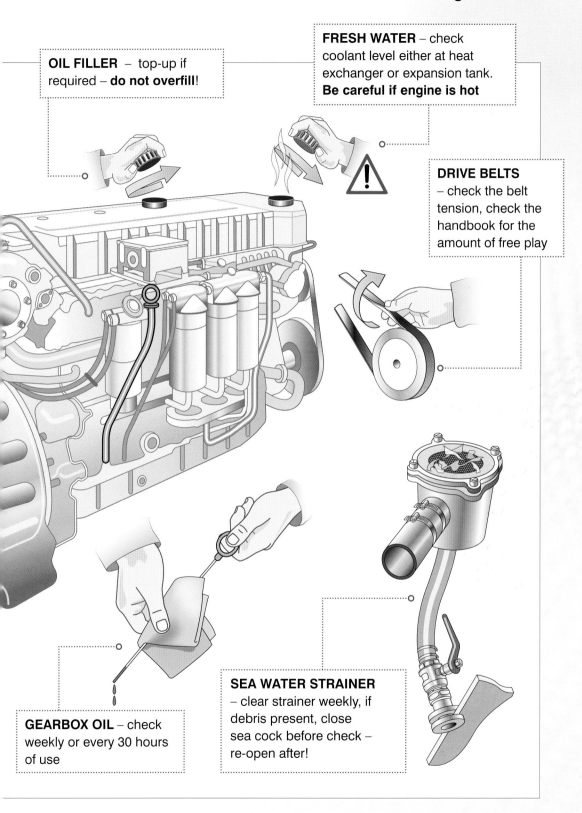

OIL FILLER – top-up if required – **do not overfill**!

FRESH WATER – check coolant level either at heat exchanger or expansion tank. **Be careful if engine is hot**

DRIVE BELTS – check the belt tension, check the handbook for the amount of free play

GEARBOX OIL – check weekly or every 30 hours of use

SEA WATER STRAINER – clear strainer weekly, if debris present, close sea cock before check – re-open after!

Control checks & going out boating

Careful consideration is required by motor boaters of weather conditions before departure. In tidal areas the speed and direction of the tidal stream must also be taken into account.

If the weather is making the voyage uncomfortable, it may well be too severe for either your, or the boat's capabilities – or both! Many factors affect wind strength and how it will impact on your boat. Consider the following rather than just the current wind strength.

■ How many days before has it been windy?

■ Is it blowing towards or away from the land you are setting off from?

■ Is the area generally sheltered from that wind direction?

■ And, most important in motor boating – is the wind with or against the tidal stream. Even a Force 4, wind against a spring tide can get rather interesting especially if in smaller craft!

Different designs of boats cope with the many differing sea conditions. A heavy displacement craft will tend to roll more but keep going happily in weather than in a faster planing craft which will have you travelling at reduced speed or slamming uncomfortably. As a leisure boater, unless in sheltered waters or wind strength below Force 5, a trip should be considered carefully before venturing out.

One of the key factors in keeping boating enjoyable is to consider the crew; make sure your boating is within theirs as well as your own comfort zone.

BEAUFORT SCALE

Beaufort Force	1	2
Wind Speed	1 – 3 Ripples	4 – 6 Small wavelets
What's it like	Great – ideal conditions	Great – still ideal

3	4	5	6+
7 – 10	11 – 16	17 – 21	22 – 27
Occasional crests	Frequent white horses	Moderate waves, many white crests	Large waves, white foam crests
Still OK	OK but getting bouncy. Smaller craft will be starting to slam	More bouncy – smaller craft may have to reduce speed	Uncomfortable for most, displacement speed, glad to see port

Safety briefing – crew

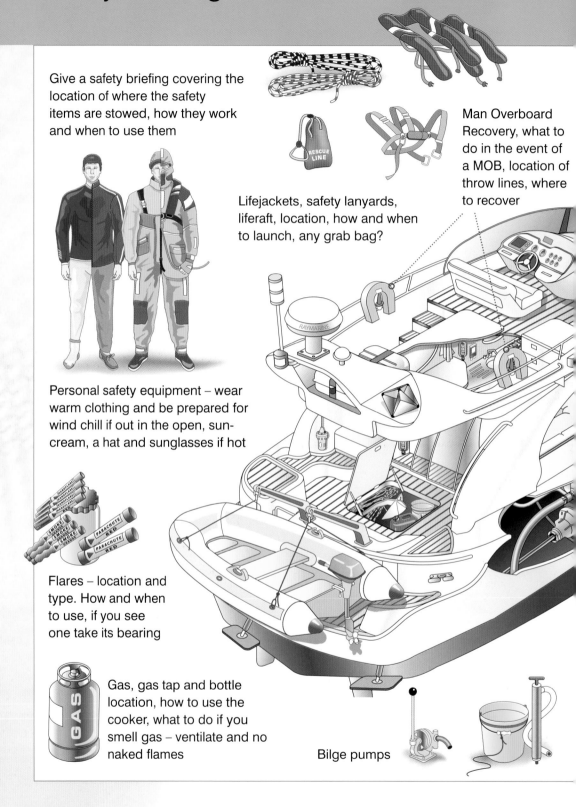

Give a safety briefing covering the location of where the safety items are stowed, how they work and when to use them

Man Overboard Recovery, what to do in the event of a MOB, location of throw lines, where to recover

Lifejackets, safety lanyards, liferaft, location, how and when to launch, any grab bag?

Personal safety equipment – wear warm clothing and be prepared for wind chill if out in the open, suncream, a hat and sunglasses if hot

Flares – location and type. How and when to use, if you see one take its bearing

Gas, gas tap and bottle location, how to use the cooker, what to do if you smell gas – ventilate and no naked flames

Bilge pumps

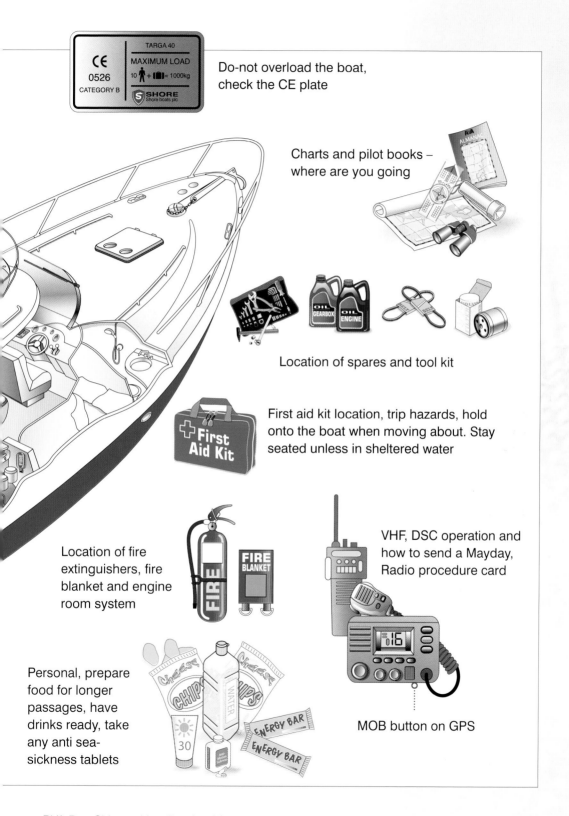

Do-not overload the boat, check the CE plate

Charts and pilot books – where are you going

Location of spares and tool kit

First aid kit location, trip hazards, hold onto the boat when moving about. Stay seated unless in sheltered water

Location of fire extinguishers, fire blanket and engine room system

VHF, DSC operation and how to send a Mayday, Radio procedure card

Personal, prepare food for longer passages, have drinks ready, take any anti sea-sickness tablets

MOB button on GPS

Handling the boat

Throttle and gear control

Most boats have combined levers so one lever controls both gear and throttle for each engine. Pushing the lever forward or backwards by one click engages gear with the engine at tick-over, further movement gives progressively more power.

Remember neutral! When changing between ahead and astern, rest the lever momentarily in neutral to reduce the chance of gearbox strain and drive train damage.

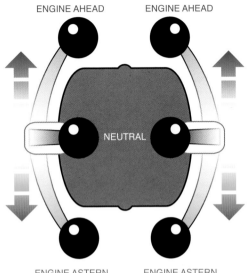

ENGINE AHEAD   ENGINE AHEAD

NEUTRAL

ENGINE ASTERN   ENGINE ASTERN

Rudders

Most craft have a way to direct the water and assist with steering – on shaft drive boats these are called rudders. To work a rudder requires water flowing over it. Flow over the rudder is gained from the propeller (called propwash), the boat moving through the water even though you may be in neutral or when a stream of water is running over the rudder.

Slow motor boats may have large rudder surface areas and are able to steer well at slow speeds. Planing craft tend to have quite small rudders so the effect is poor at slow speed.

When you turn the rudder and engage gear it throws propwash over one side of the rudder. This increases the rudder's effectiveness and turns the boat in a smaller circle.

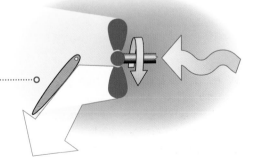

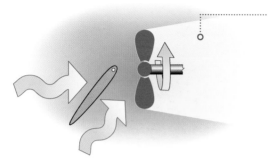

When going astern, water is pulled over the rudder's surface by the prop but the propwash does not flow across the rudders, as the wash is going under the boat. The result is that steering relies more on water flow gained by movement astern.

Pivot Points

When a boat turns, the bow goes one way and the stern the other. Because of the position of the rudders it is actually the stern of the boat that is being steered even though the bow is also turning.

Ahead

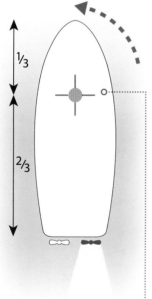

Astern

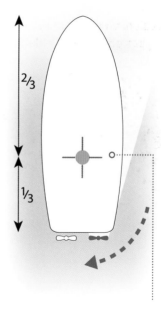

When going ahead, the boat pivots around a point approximately a third in from the bow. When turning in ahead beware of colliding with obstructions with your stern.

When going astern, the pivot point moves to a position approximately a third in from the stern, watch the bow as this will swing in a greater arc.

Handling the boat

Pivot points

When manoeuvring in tight spaces, turn the rudder first and then apply power. The propwash from the propeller will deflect off the angled rudder and turns the boat in a smaller space.

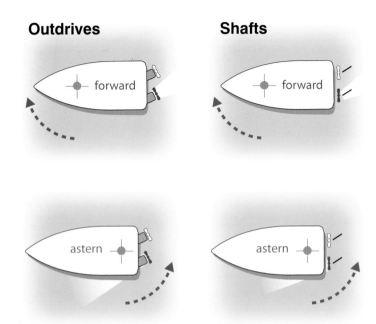

Outdrives

forward

astern

Shafts

forward

astern

Propellers

Propellers push the boat through the water, and are either right or left handed. This is determined by the leading edge of the blade when viewed from behind. In forward gear this prop would spin or twist right-handed (clockwise) and in astern would spin anti-clockwise.

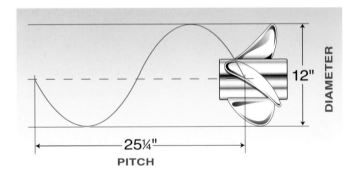

12"

DIAMETER

25¼"

PITCH

Pitch and diameter

Props are measured by their pitch and diameter.
- Diameter is the actual diameter of the propeller and blades and usually increases with engine size.
- Pitch is the theoretical distance the craft will travel on one rotation of the propeller. The actual distance travelled will be less due to slippage.

Propwalk

Propellers push the boat forward, but because of their rotation they also make the stern move to one side. This effect is called propwalk, it is most noticeable when going astern. Nearly all boats have propwalk and prop and hull design play a large part in how much.

Single screw boats

Propwalk – Ahead

All boats are designed to go forward, and the hull shape helps to reduce propwalk so it's easy to drive the streamlined shape ahead. However propwalk is still there and a right-handed prop will try to walk the stern to starboard as well as drive the boat forward when going ahead.

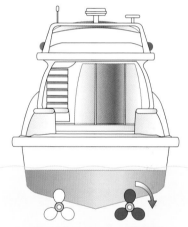
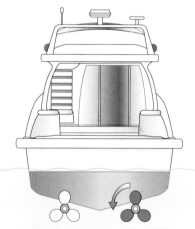

Right-hand prop AHEAD   Right-hand prop ASTERN

Propwalk – Astern

In astern a right-handed prop will walk the stern to port. Propwalk is always much more noticeable in astern as the blunter stern shape means that less push from the propeller will be translated into astern movement and it will have a more noticeable kick to port.

> **TIP** You can check for propwalk when tied alongside. Ensure the rudder is straight, engage astern gear and observe which side the wash comes out from under the hull and the boat will kick the other way. This is really useful to know before attempting to manoeuvre the boat.

Handling the boat

Twin screw boats

Most have twin contra-rotating propellers, placed equidistant from the centre line thus creating a turning effect called offset turning.

Generally, when viewed from astern, both screws are outward turning. When both engines are in ahead or astern this makes the boat move ahead or astern; individually in gear ahead or astern, they will reinforce the pivot action and increase the rate of turn.

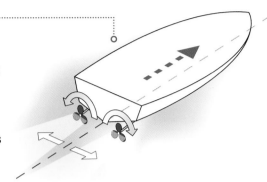

Twin engine boats are especially manoeuvrable, as shown in this example:

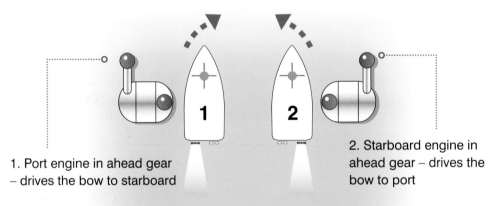

1. Port engine in ahead gear – drives the bow to starboard

2. Starboard engine in ahead gear – drives the bow to port

Both engines ahead – drives straight.

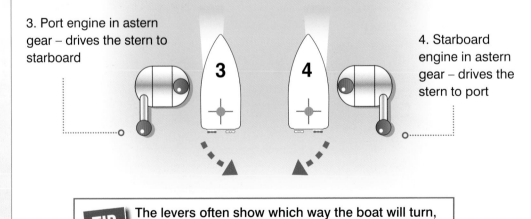

3. Port engine in astern gear – drives the stern to starboard

4. Starboard engine in astern gear – drives the stern to port

> **TIP** The levers often show which way the boat will turn, just remember the pivot points!

Outdrives

Are a very efficient way of transmitting engine power into thrust as the whole outdrive leg is steerable giving directional thrust. This makes the boat very manoeuvrable. But as there is no rudder you will have to steer and then apply power to make the system effective. They can have single or duoprops; duoprops have no propwalk because the contra-rotating props cancel each other out.

As the drives are at the stern of the boat the pivot point moves further forward when in ahead, and further aft when in astern.

Twin outdrives are generally closer together than shafts, this combined with generally smaller propellers means that the offset turning effect and any propwalk are both reduced,

TIP	The best manoeuvrability is achieved by turning the helm before engaging gear – hence the term 'No Gear – No Steer'. On twin engine boats the outside engine will give the maximum leverage.

Bow thrusters

Found on modern boats and used when the boat is stationary to push the bows to one side. The stern will move to the other side as the boat pivots around the centre. They are best used in short bursts and you usually push the control the direction you want the bow to move.

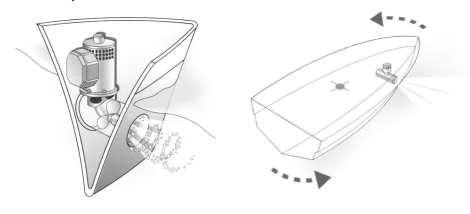

Wind and stream both affect a boat's handling and you need to be especially aware of both when manoeuvring around harbours and marinas.

■ Planing craft tend to have a lot of windage combined with poorer grip on the water.

■ Semi and displacement craft tend to be less affected by the wind but more so by stream.

Wind

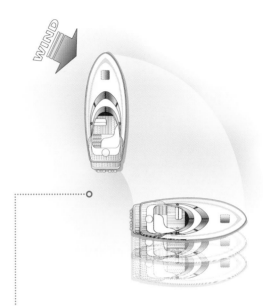

Watch for wind direction, it can be seen on the water's surface, but more obvious indicators are flags, yacht mast indicators and feeling it on your face.

Motor boats tend to have less grip on the bow so are easily affected by the wind. Left alone most motor boats usually lie abeam to the wind and drift sideways.

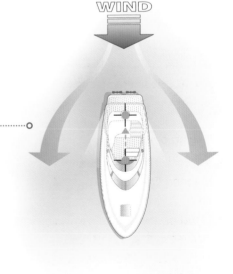

When waiting in a motorboat the easiest position is stern-to the wind, you can then engage astern to hold position. Since going astern moves the pivot point aft, it helps the stern seek the wind with the bow positioned downwind.

Stream

The effect of either tide, natural river flow or some locks. Stream has the effect of moving all objects in one direction. Heavier objects take longer for it to take effect but when they have gained momentum, they take longer to stop.

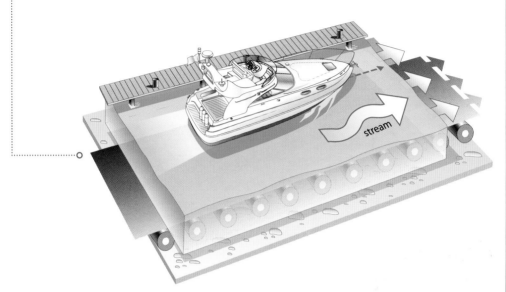

If you motor in the same direction as the stream, your boat travels faster and you will arrive quicker. If you motor into the stream you will take longer to arrive as you will be moving slower over the ground. Manoeuvring into stream gives you greater control of the boat.

You can assess any stream by looking at

- Bubbles or weed in the water flowing past a boat.
- Moored boats leaving a wake.
- Mooring lines pulled tight at one end.
- Weed on the pontoon flowing downstream.
- Water stacking up around stationary objects.

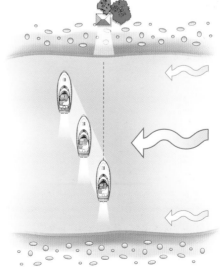

Power handling

Turning – single engine
When turning always consider the elements first, try to turn into the strongest element.

Turning in wind
Drive into the gap – use the wind to assist by turning the bow through the wind. Put the rudder hard over and give a short burst of power, next use astern to give room, then keep the bow moving and drive out.

Use of propwalk
The effect of propwalk will either help or hinder a turn in wind. If possible turn by using propwalk.

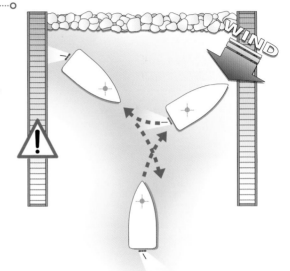

Turning in stream
When turning with a stream running through a marina aisle, turn the bow through the stream.

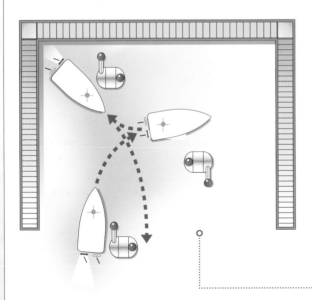

Turning – twin engines
Twin engines make the boat more manoeuvrable and can be turned in three ways.

1. The simplest method is to use one engine at a time. The outside engine gives the greatest leverage and turning power and will give a slow gentle turn.

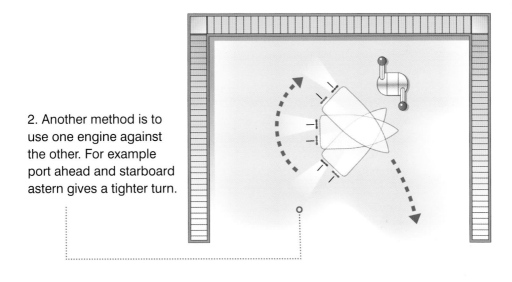

2. Another method is to use one engine against the other. For example port ahead and starboard astern gives a tighter turn.

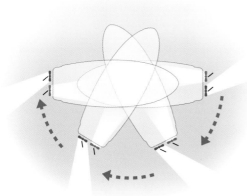

3. The tightest turn can be achieved by using split throttles with the rudders turned to assist the ahead engine. **Remember to straighten the helm after.**

Tight turning

For a tighter turn, start from very slow or stopped. Remember, speed carried into a turn increases the turning circle and makes the boat slide sideways, increasing the radius.

- Helm hard over with a burst ahead, turn the bow through the wind. Once the bow is through the wind it will help turn the boat.
- Engage neutral, go astern to stop forward momentum and gain some room. The rudder can be left in the same position as you will probably not gain enough speed astern to steer.
- Back to neutral, a burst ahead keeps the boat turning. When pointing in the right direction, straighten the helm and drive out.

Power handling

Outdrive and Outboard boats

As outdrives use vectored propwash from the propellers rather than rudders, helm needs to be used to achieve the best manoeuvrability. This works best if the wheel is turned before gear is engaged, otherwise valuable space will be lost in forward or astern movement, known as wheel before gear. On a twin engine boat, as the propellers are generally closer together than on shaft driven, splitting the throttle does not usually give as great a turning momentum as using a single engine at a time after turning the wheel. So turning particularly in a confined space is achieved by following a simple order: **Neutral** – **turn** wheel – **ahead** – **neutral** – **reverse** wheel – **astern** – **neutral**, repeating until the turn is completed. The following illustrations make this easy to understand.

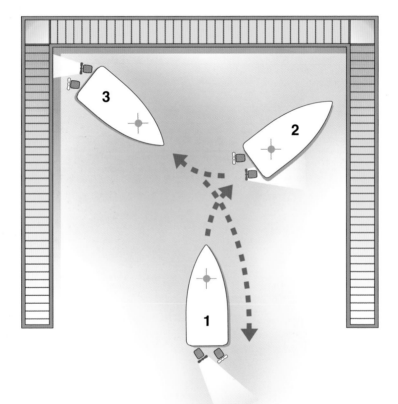

Remember, motor slowly into space and slow the boat

1. Wheel hard to starboard. Ahead port engine, monitor the space ·······························o

o·············· **2. Neutral as gap closes. Wheel hard to port. Astern starboard engine. Monitor the space**

3. Neutral as gap closes. Wheel hard to starboard. Ahead port engine. Monitor the space. Drive out when straight. ··············o

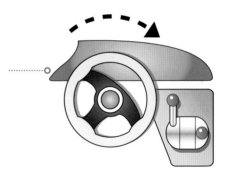

You will see that the engine used is the opposite to the helm movement, this rule works in both ahead and astern. If on a single outdrive boat then the wheel movements are the same, just use the single engine.

> **TIP** Pivot points on outdrive boats are closer to the extremities, this is especially noticeable in astern and the bow can drift very quickly in a crosswind.

Berthing

Motor at the slowest speed which allows control to be maintained – usually tick-over in gear. The greatest skill is in assessing the strength and direction of any wind and stream so that you start in the correct place and if you communicate the plan effectively to the crew, you greatly increase your chance of success.

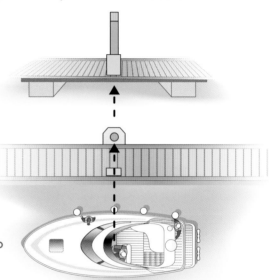

Speed
Judge your speed relative to the pontoon you intend to berth against. Best done by looking to the side and judging how quickly you pass cleats, piles, or moored boats.

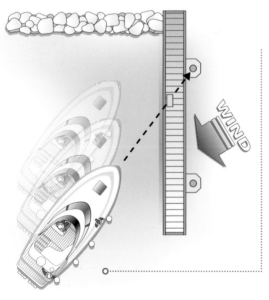

Drift
The wind may well be blowing you on or off your intended berth. To judge which way and by how much you can use a transit (two fixed objects on land in line):

- If being blown away from the pontoon, you will need to aim slightly earlier at your intended berth to counteract its force.
- If you are being blown on to the berth, aim slightly past your berth so you do not land too early.

Basic approaches

There are three approaches in an ideal scenario.
1 – No wind or tide. 2 – Onshore wind. 3 – Offshore wind.

1. No wind or tide

- Aim for a point at the front of the berth.
- Approach at a shallow angle.
- Use neutral to control speed.
- When close, drive the bow away from the berth, this will also bring the stern in closer.

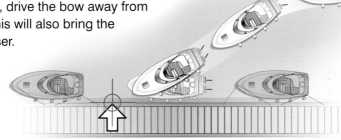

- Use a burst astern to stop the boat. If a twin engined boat, the outside engine will slow you and help walk the stern in.

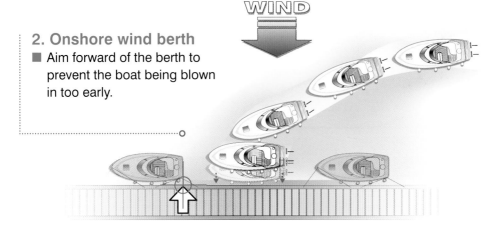

2. Onshore wind berth

- Aim forward of the berth to prevent the boat being blown in too early.

- To counteract arriving too early, steer away from the pontoon and drive ahead to keep the boat parallel with the intended berth.
- Just as the fenders are about to touch, stop the boat and let the wind finish blowing you onto the berth. If you have a bow thruster this can help you land in style.

Berthing

3. Gentle offshore wind berth
Requires a more positive approach so fender appropriately.
1. Aim at a steeper angle towards the beginning of the berth.
2. About a metre (3ft) away, steer parallel to the berth.
   The boat's momentum will help continue the slide
   towards the berth.
3. As the boat is parallel get the lines
   ashore promptly and stop the
   boat.

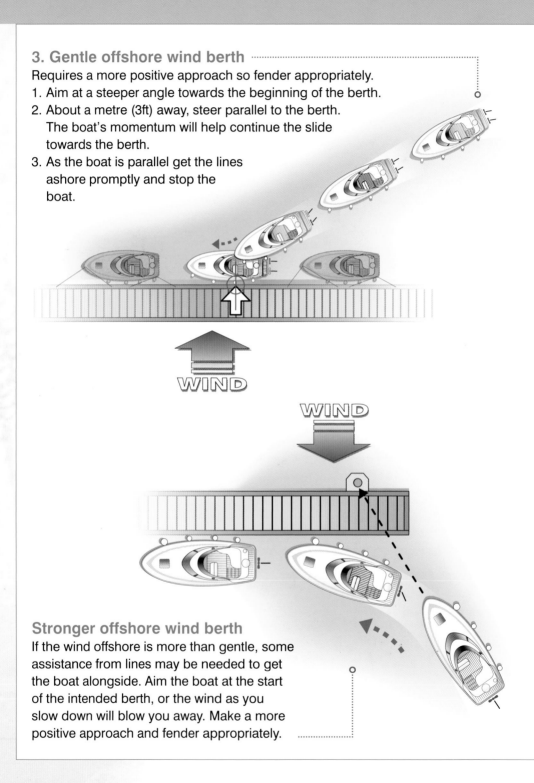

Stronger offshore wind berth
If the wind offshore is more than gentle, some
assistance from lines may be needed to get
the boat alongside. Aim the boat at the start
of the intended berth, or the wind as you
slow down will blow you away. Make a more
positive approach and fender appropriately.

Single screw

You may find lines (as in the illustration below) help make the manoeuvre easier.

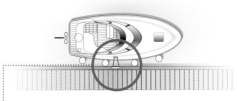 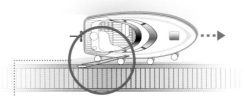

A line from a mid-ships cleat will hold the boat alongside while the others are being tied off.

You can also motor gently ahead on a line rigged from a mid-ships cleat to hold the boat alongside.

Twin shafts and outdrives

1. Approach as slowly as maintaining steerage allows. Position the boat at a balance point where you can hold it steady against any wind.
2. Using a bow line lasso the cleat by the bow and tie the line off securely.
3. Now go astern on the outside engine, if it's windy you can aid the twist by going ahead on the inside engine and steer away from the dock if very windy.

This reduces the load on the cleats and is essential on a larger boat. Outdrives usually just need to go astern on the outside engine because they can steer towards (or away) from the dock speeding up or slowing down the rate the stern closes.

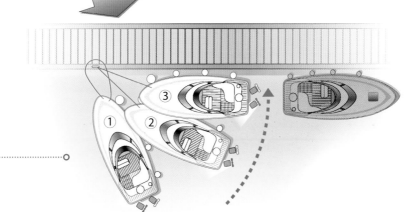

Berthing

Securing the boat

Good communication makes this task so much easier. Make a plan, advise the crew of what's expected. If unsure of the best approach, drawing a simple sketch may help.

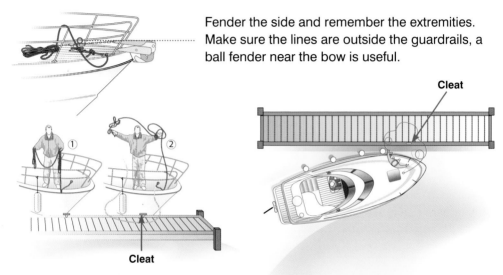

Fender the side and remember the extremities. Make sure the lines are outside the guardrails, a ball fender near the bow is useful.

- Sometimes lassoing is the easiest way to get a line ashore.
- Ensure that the crew don't obstruct your view.
- Get crew to call or indicate the distance from the boat to the land – **don't jump!**

Berthing into a stream

- Aim at the forward end of the berth.
- Use a shallow angle of approach.
- When in position, increase the angle, then use the stream to slide the boat sideways onto the berth.

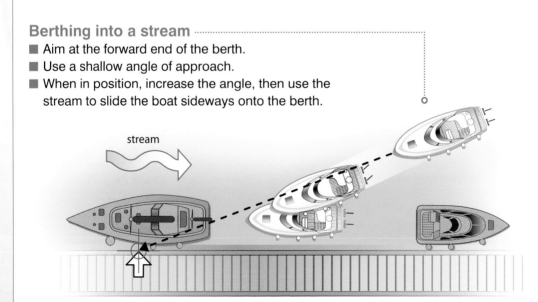

Caution
Aim too close to the downstream vessel and your boat's stern may collide with it.

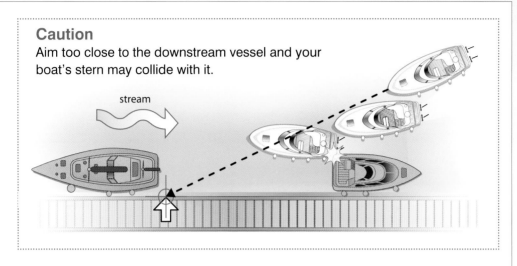

Berthing in a stream
Any stream can make berthing much easier, and is a key factor in your planning.

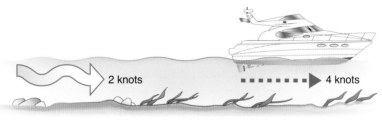

stream 2 knots + boat 4 knots = total 6 knots

If you approach with the stream, your boat is going faster relative to the pontoon than it needs to!

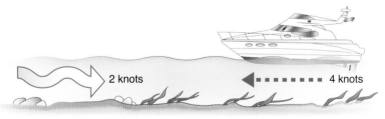

boat 4 knots - stream 2 knots = total 2 knots

If you approach into the stream, you can maintain the slowest approach and greatest control as you have more water flow over the rudders or outdrives; remember – judge speed by looking abeam.

Berthing

Ferry gliding

A very simple but useful technique, the boat moves sideways by using the elements. Works easily with a good wind in stream and if your boat has a lot of windage in a good wind.

You need to angle the boat so that there is more element (stream or wind) on one side than the other, whilst keeping forward motion to a minimum. When you want to stop sideways movement you simply make the boat parallel with the element (called stemming). To move sideways again, adjust the helm so that you present more of one side to the element, whilst keeping speed slow.

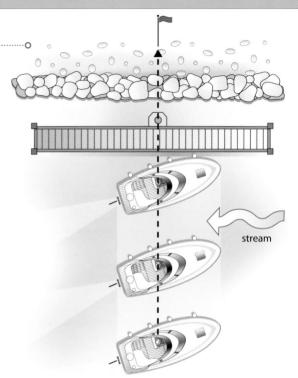

stream

Downstream berthing

Not easy as boats have no natural elements to use as brakes and as the boat slows you can lose control. When approaching a downstream berth keep a shallow angle and get the stern line on first. Better still go slightly past the berth, then you can approach into the elements stern first.

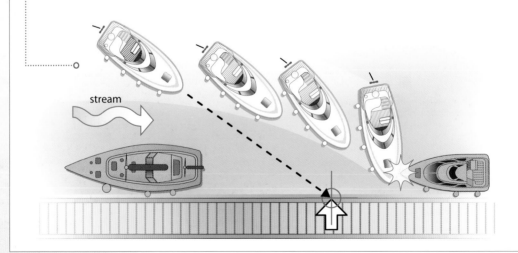

stream

Mooring to a harbour wall

- Check depth – if tidal, check fall of tide at low water!
- Remember you may need to adjust your lines from on the boat.
- Moor temporarily to the ladder whilst you get sorted.
- Use a fender board if the wall is uneven.
- If there is a tidal range your lines need to be three times the range.

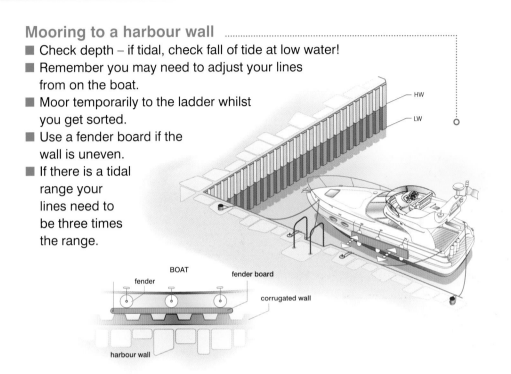

Rafting up

- In some harbours, you may need to raft up to other boats.
- It's polite to ask adjoining boats first – if they are aboard! Put your fenders higher – on the gunwale.
- Try to raft to a boat of similar size and check beforehand when they intend leaving.
- Try to have the boats facing the same way.
- When you have tied up, walk your shore lines ashore by walking round the bow, not through the other boat's cockpit.

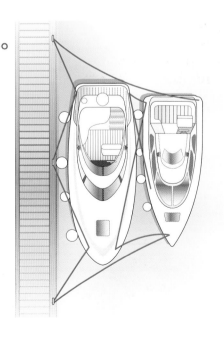

Tying the boat up

When your day is finished some simple steps will keep your boat better maintained and a pleasure to use next time.

Let the engines cool by having a period of reduced revs before you switch off

Re-connect the shore power if needed

Check the engine compartment for any leaks

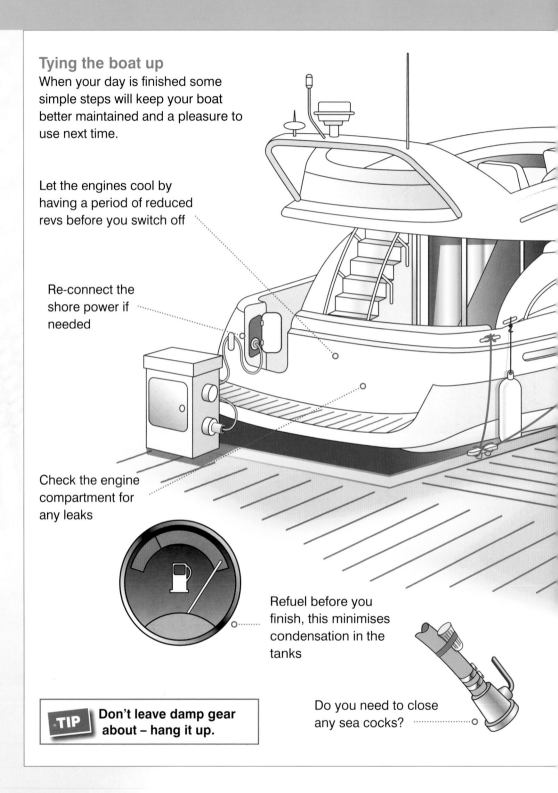

Refuel before you finish, this minimises condensation in the tanks

Do you need to close any sea cocks?

TIP **Don't leave damp gear about – hang it up.**

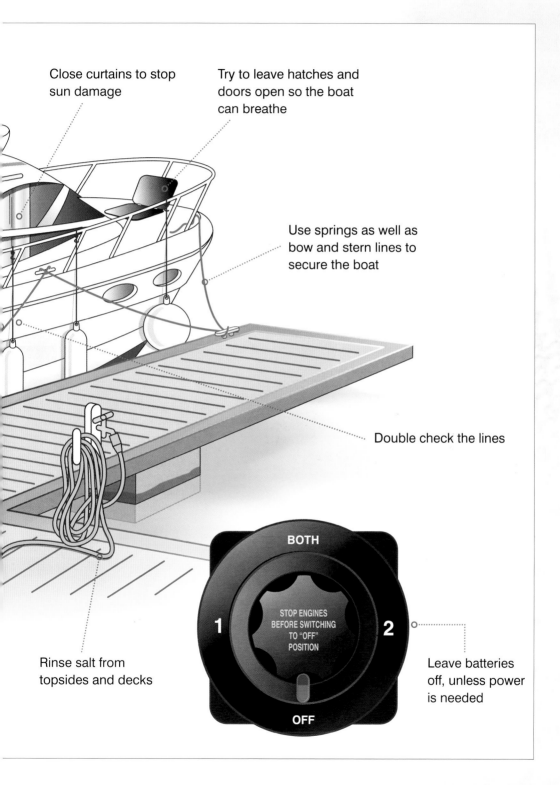

Close curtains to stop sun damage

Try to leave hatches and doors open so the boat can breathe

Use springs as well as bow and stern lines to secure the boat

Double check the lines

Rinse salt from topsides and decks

BOTH

STOP ENGINES BEFORE SWITCHING TO "OFF" POSITION

1

2

OFF

Leave batteries off, unless power is needed

Leaving a berth

The shape of a motor boat and where it pivots means that it is often easier to leave in astern. Once the stern is in clear water you can motor away from the dock. In gentle conditions the following techniques work well.

Single screw
1. You will almost certainly need to motor out in astern.
2. Fender the bow well.
3. Turn the helm towards the dock.
4. Engage tick-over ahead to push the bow in.
5. When the stern is in clear water, select neutral.
6. Straighten the helm and motor astern.

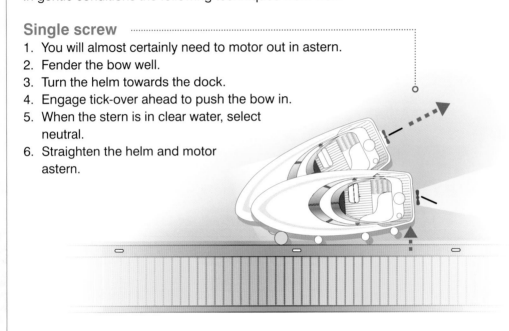

Twin screw
1. Fender the bow well.
2. Go astern on the inside engine. The stern will be pivoted away from the dock and the boat will move gently astern.
3. Once the stern is away, the other engine can also be used to straighten the boat.

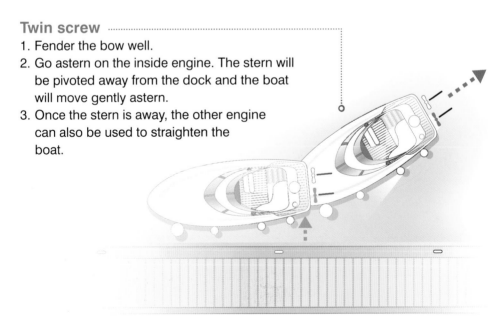

Twin outdrives

Outdrives by their very nature require a slightly different technique.

1. Normally we use the rule of opposites but now,
2. Steer away from the dock and go astern on the outside engine (in this example wheel to port and port engine astern); this lifts the boat from the dock.

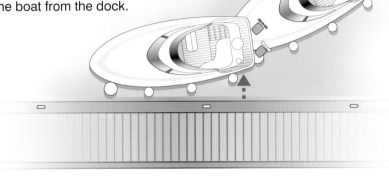

Bow thrusters

If you have a bow thruster it can be a great aid. Sadly they are not always powerful enough to push the bow through the wind on a windy day.

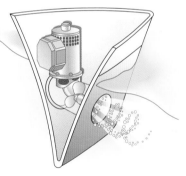

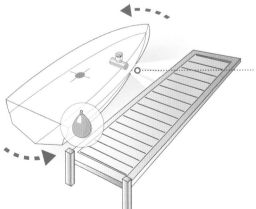

1. Simply push the bow off the dock with the thruster.
2. When far enough off
3. Go ahead to motor clear – watch the stern and remember to fender it well as it will be pushed towards the dock as the bow is pushed out.

Leaving a berth

Leaving with an offshore wind

An offshore wind will happily blow you away from the berth, you just need to control the exit!

1. Rig slip lines, pick a transit so you don't drift fore or aft.
2. Slip the stern line first as the bow will drift faster.
3. When clear, motor away.

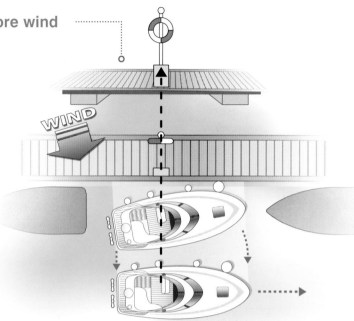

Leaving with an onshore wind

How you can use lines to help leave.

Twin screw and outdrive

1. Rig a slip line from the bow, going ahead of the boat.
2. Use tick-over astern on the inside engine to tension it and pull the stern into clear water.
3. When happy, engage neutral, slip the line and continue to motor away.

- If very windy you can use the inside engine astern and the outside ahead to pivot away more positively.
- If using an outdrive turn the wheel away from the dock to increase the turning effort.
- Single outdrives can use the same technique.

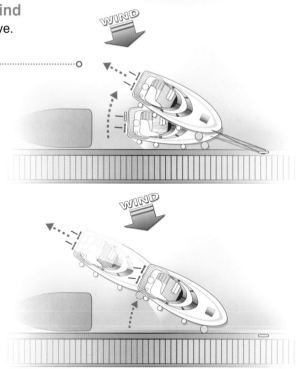

Single screw

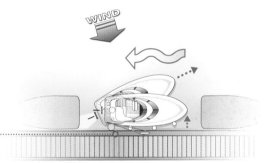

With an onshore wind single screw boats need to motor against a spring to get the stern into clear water.

1. Rig a bow spring on a slip line. Make sure it's outside any rails and will run free when released.
2. Slip all other lines.
3. Now gently motor ahead.
4. When the stern is clear, engage neutral.
5. Slip the spring line and motor away in astern.

 TIP This technique can be used by twin engined boats but take care as the pivot point will be different and the bow can snub in.

Using springs in stream

The big decision here is which spring to use? The answer is quite simple – always the one where the stream will help push the boat away from the dock.

1. If the stream is on the bow, then use a stern spring.
2. If using a stern spring, then fender the stern well, especially if your boat is rather square as it will be vulnerable when you go ahead. If twin engined, by making your first movement ahead with the engine furthest from the dock, you stand less chance of damage.
3. If the stream is on the stern then use a bow spring.

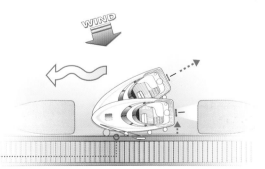

Marinas

Marinas are often crowded with relatively tight spaces that present no great problems on gentle days, however if it's windy or there is lots of stream, take extra care and be aware of the dangers. You need to think much further ahead.

Be aware to which side of the aisle the boat is being pushed (the downwind side) and think of this as the danger side; this makes the other side the safe side so stay towards the (safe) upwind side for greater safety and a longer period of time to react.

Leaving a berth
When leaving a berth, beware of being blown onto surrounding craft, so use slip lines and exit the berth positively and ensure the stern is clear before tuning.

Arriving
On arrival you may well need to position the boat so that all of the berth will become visible on the final approach, called making it open.
- This may entail going past and turning round.
- Try to use the wind as a brake for the bow, so you don't get blown around.
- Have lines and fenders ready.
- Be prepared to fender both sides in case you get blown onto a neighbouring boat.

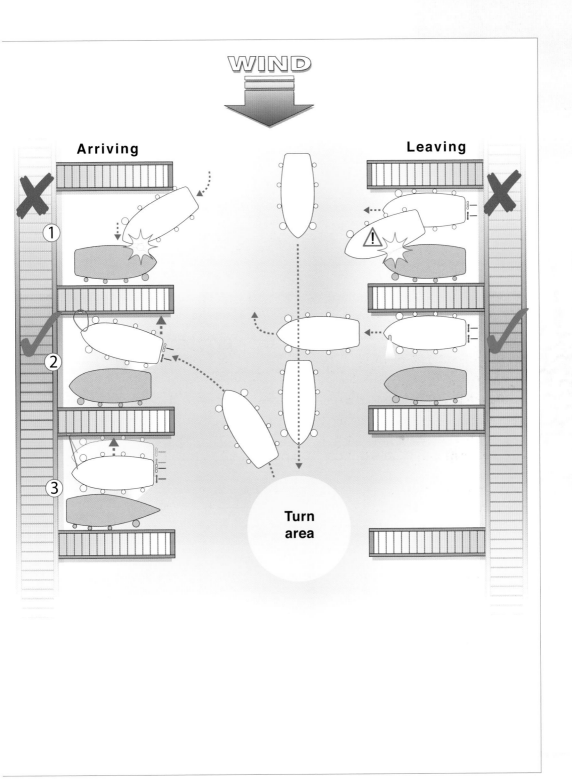

WIND

Arriving

Leaving

Turn area

Stern-to and bow-to mooring

Many areas around the world berth bow or stern to the quay, with an anchor and a line to hold the boat off the quay.

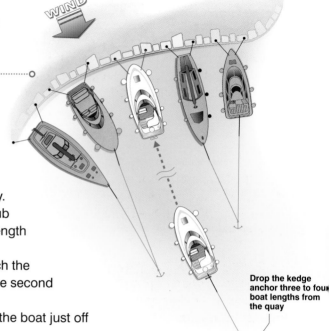

Bow-to

1. Prepare the bow lines and fender both sides.
2. If using a kedge anchor at the stern, prepare it and ensure it is tied on.
3. Drop the kedge three to four boat lengths from the quay.
4. Keep moving forward, then snub the kedge anchor half a boat length off.
5. Stop just off the quay and attach the windward bow line first, then the second one.
6. Now tighten the kedge to hold the boat just off the quay.

Drop the kedge anchor three to four boat lengths from the quay

Lazy Lines

If the harbour uses lazy lines, then the approach is similar but with no need to use an anchor. Instead use the lazy line which is a line attached to a permanent mooring line on the harbour bed. You just pull and tighten the attached stern line to hold you off the quay.

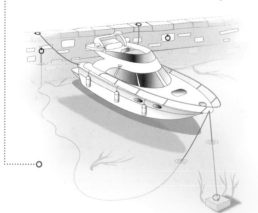

Stern-to

Usually offers easier access to the shore but less privacy. Be especially careful as it may be shallow just at the harbour wall which could be especially damaging to your stern gear.

For a stern-to berth
1. Prepare two stern lines, fender both sides and the transom.
2. Prepare the anchor.
3. Reverse in and drop the kedge three to four boat lengths from the quay.
4. Keep moving back, then snub the anchor half a boat length off.
5. Stop just off the quay and attach the stern windward first, then the second one.
6. Now tighten the anchor rode to hold the boat just off the quay.

Offshore wind
An offshore wind makes the whole process easier as it holds the boat steady whilst the stern will seek the wind.

If the wind is across the quay, then reverse towards it and drop the anchor just before you turn towards your berth.

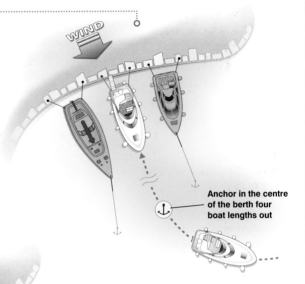

Anchor in the centre of the berth four boat lengths out

Onshore wind
This can tricky as the bows want to blow off. However once the anchor is down it will help hold the bows head to wind.
- Now tension the anchor and then ease it out as you move astern.
- Take care with the power as if the anchor drags you could hit the wall.

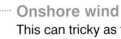

Mooring buoys

Mooring buoys require good communication between the helm and foredeck crew. The helm may lose sight of the mooring buoy as you get close so the crew need to give direction and distance. Always approach into the strongest element – you can do a dummy run so that you can judge which will be the best approach, and what type of buoy it is. The best angle of approach is often given by how other boats are lying in the area.

In the illustration, the mooring buoy has a pick-up buoy to make things easier, this you simply lift but it may have a light line on it connected to a heavier line that you place over your cleat. If this is too large for your boat, then place a smaller line through it which you attach to your own cleats.

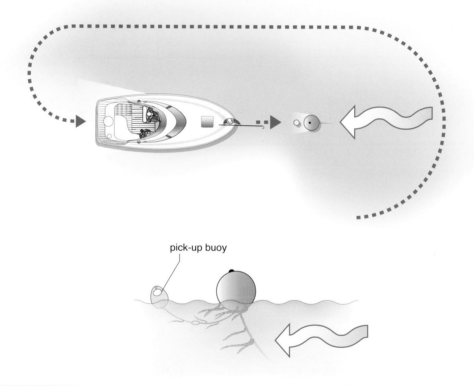

pick-up buoy

TIP If approaching with a crosswind, stay slightly upwind to allow for drift as you slow down. You need to keep the boat still whilst the crew catch the pick-up buoy.

Lasso

If there is not a pick-up buoy, then you may need to lasso the buoy to attach the boat, you will then have more time to connect a line to the ring on top.

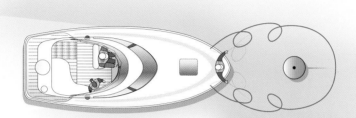

 A good idea is to have all crew practise throwing a lasso.

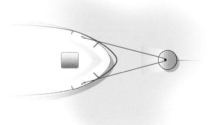

Never rely on a lasso alone as it could pull the buoy off the chain, or the chain could wear through your line. If more than a short stay consider placing a second line for extra security.

Anchoring

- Select your anchorage with care, study the weather forecast.
- It needs be sheltered from the present wind direction and any changes which may happen whilst you are anchored.
- Always have an escape route which needs to work for day and night.
- If there are other boats, observe how they are lying, this will give a clue as to your best approach.
- If in tidal waters, you need to consider the rise and fall of the tide during your stay.

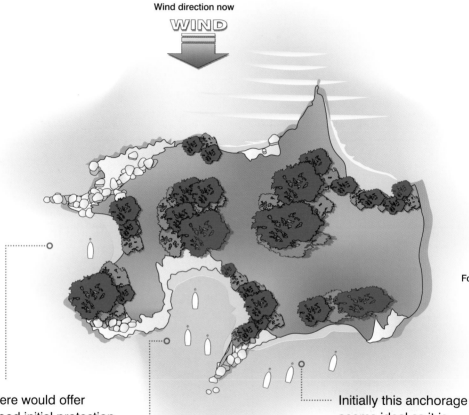

Wind direction now

WIND

Forecast wind direction

Here would offer good initial protection and still be fine later with the forecast wind. Also offers a good escape route if the weather changes quickly.

Here offers better shelter to start with and would be good in the forecast wind. However it would become a lee shore if the wind continued to move round.

Initially this anchorage seems ideal as it is sheltered from the wind. But it may be prone to swell coming round the headland and would only need a small change of wind direction to become uncomfortable.

Dropping the anchor

- If using a powered windlass (winch) make sure it is turned on.
- Head the boat into the strongest element (wind or stream) and then bring it to a halt.
- Keep stationary whilst you lower the anchor to the sea bed.
- Continue to lower the chain as the boat drifts back on the elements, (in light conditions you may need a touch of astern).
- Once the correct amount of chain is lowered engage astern to pull the chain taut and check holding.
- Transfer the load on the winch to a cleat or other strong point.

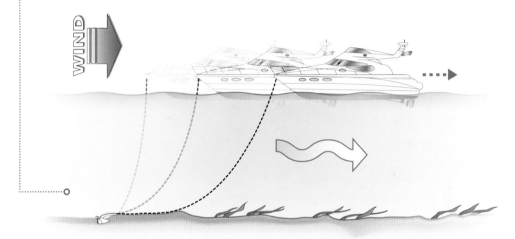

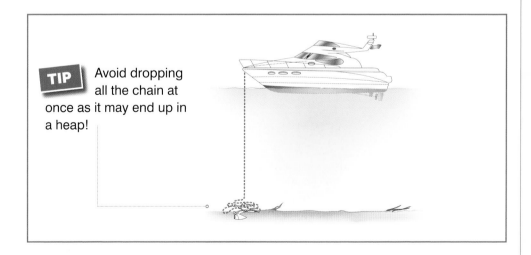

TIP Avoid dropping all the chain at once as it may end up in a heap!

Anchoring

Are you holding?

- Once the anchor is down, find a transit to monitor your position.
- Use an anchor alarm on the GPS – don't make the alarm circle too big.
- Monitor the depth on the echo sounder.
- If in an area you don't know, then consider a tripping line so that you can retrieve the anchor if it gets stuck.

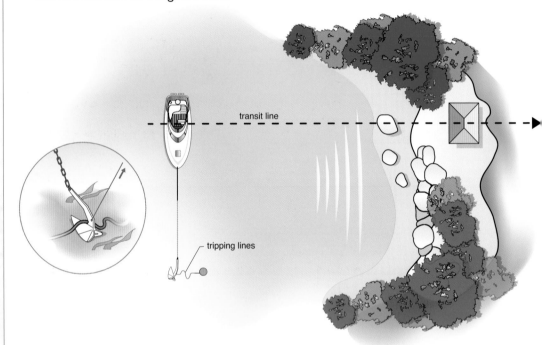

Scope

You need to be aware of how much chain and/or rope to let out, with all chain 4 x the depth would be sufficient. With a chain and rope combination, then 6 x the depth. You really want at least 10m (33ft) of chain with a combination. Remember to allow for any rise and fall of tide.

Remember also that if you let out lots of scope, the boat will swing in a greater arc as the wind or stream changes.

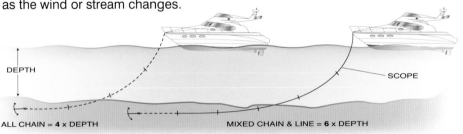

Weighing Anchor

1. Get the engines running as the winch uses lots of power.

2. When ready to leave get a crew member to point in the direction the chain is lying – so you know where to steer.

3. Hand signals to the crew are good especially if it is windy.

4. Go gently ahead to take the boat's weight off the winch.

5. Winch up, monitoring the strain on the winch, motor forward again if the pressure is too great.

6. When the anchor is aboard stow it carefully and switch off the winch.

What if it's stuck?
1. If stuck, usually a direct pull upwards frees it.
2. If not, secure the chain and motor gently ahead to pull it out at the opposite angle to how it went in.

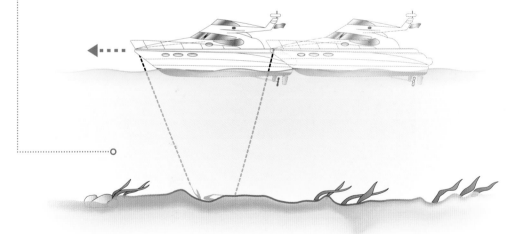

Going to sea

Safe speed

Before you leave the confines of the harbour, ensure you have stowed all clutter.

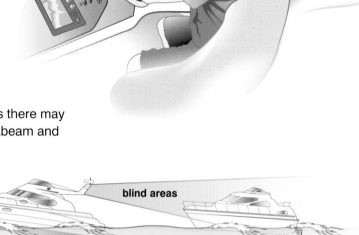

- Consider what speed you will be travelling, at 20 knots you travel a mile every 3 minutes, so you need to be thinking a long way ahead.
- Travel at a speed that you can think at!
- If helming from inside be especially vigilant as there may be blind spots, watch abeam and astern as well.

blind areas

blind areas

- Adjust your speed to the conditions, especially if visibility is poor.
- If on a planing boat, your view astern is very poor.
- Use the radar to assist you.
- Keep a good watch for fishing markers or marker buoys.
- Consider slowing down at night.

As a boater you must be fully aware of your responsibility to each other. As a motor boater you must consider your wash and the speed at which you can travel, as this can catch out small and slower craft. Be aware that sailing boats often change course (tack) to reach their destination, be patient as this can catch out the unwary.

Collision avoidance

The International Regulations for Preventing Collisions at Sea (IRPCS) govern what we do afloat and they can be simply expressed as...

■ You have a responsibility to observe the rules.

■ Keep a good lookout at all times.

■ Use a safe speed for the conditions and traffic density and depth at all times.

■ Assess the risk of collision early.

■ If you are the give way (stand off) vessel, make your intentions clear and in plenty of time.

■ Even if the stand on vessel, monitor the other vessel.

Is there a risk of collision?

A risk of collision exists if another vessel is on a steady bearing, this can be judged in many ways.

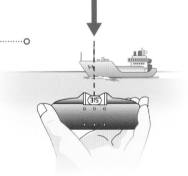

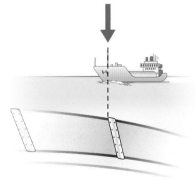

A compass, either hand bearing or fitted can be used to assess the bearing. If the bearing does not change you will collide.

Use a part of your boat to line up with the other vessel. If it stays lined up (a steady bearing) you will collide.

Going to sea

Radar

Using radar – the EBL (electronic bearing line) can be placed on the target; if it remains on the line you will collide. If it falls behind the line you will pass ahead, if it moves ahead of the line you will pass behind.

Remember for big ships in open sea 1 mile is CLOSE!

Some common scenarios you will come across.

Head on

Each vessel must make a clear and obvious turn to starboard in order to pass port to port. If there is no risk of collision, well clear craft can pass starboard to starboard.

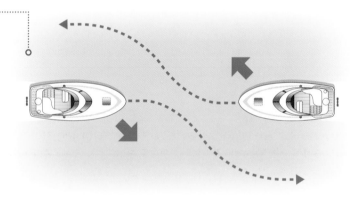

Crossing situation

At sea give way is to the right.

- The stand on vessel should hold its course and speed while continuing to monitor what action the other vessel is taking.
- The stand off (give way) vessel should alter its course and apply speed to stay clear of the other vessel.

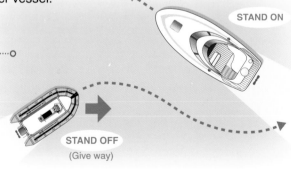

STAND ON

STAND OFF
(Give way)

Give way or stand on?

You are the give way vessel if you see another vessel approaching from the starboard side. If it is approaching from the port (the left) then you are the stand on vessel.

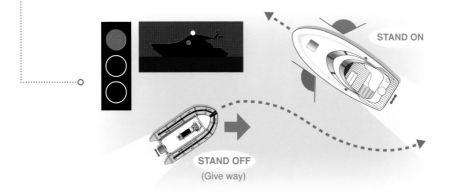

Overtaking

An overtaking vessel (one that falls in the overtaking arc) must keep clear and not impede the vessel they are overtaking. The vessel being overtaken must maintain its course and speed.

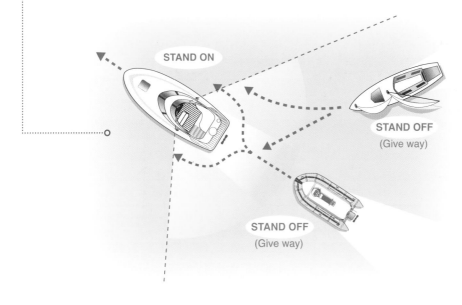

Going to sea

Narrow channels

Narrow channels are ones which other vessels can only manoeuvre within and may appear to be like open water when outside the harbour to a small boat. But larger craft are really constrained in narrow channels. Common sense dictates that if you are able to travel outside these waters then it is not only safer but you will not cause concern to other users.

In general you need to:

- Cross the narrow channel at right angles.
- Keep clear of large vessels constrained by their draught and do not impede their passage.
- If it is deep enough, use the water outside the main channel.

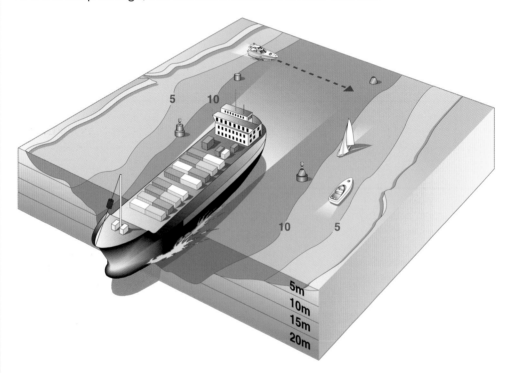

Giving way to vessel – under sail and others

Unless in a narrow channel relative to your size or being overtaken, boats under power must give way to sail powered vessels.

You must give way to vessels **Not Under Command (NUC), Constrained By Draft (CBD), Restricted in Ability to Manoeuvre (RAM)** and lastly fishing vessels which are fishing.

Sailing vessels are often moving at the behest of the wind which controls the direction they are taking. Having an awareness of which way they are likely to turn is a great advantage. Unable to sail directly towards the wind they have to tack.

When sailing vessels meet, which way they turn is again governed by whether they are the stand on or give way vessels. This is determined by which tack they are on, this is dictated by which side of the boat the wind is blowing. Wind coming over the starboard side (sails

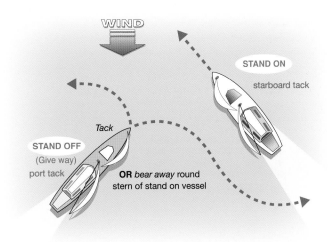

on port side) = starboard tack. Wind coming over the port side (sails on starboard side) = port tack.

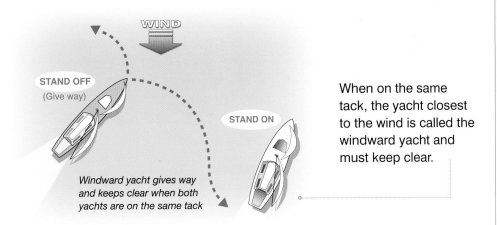

When on the same tack, the yacht closest to the wind is called the windward yacht and must keep clear.

Restricted visibility

In restricted visibility, for example heavy rain or fog, then you all become give way vessels.
- Proceed at slow speed.
- Use all available means of lookout, including sound and radar.
- Consider heading towards shallow water where there are no large vessels.

Lights, shapes and sounds

At night, vessels display navigation lights to indicate which type of vessel. The position of the lights helps indicate the vessel's direction. By day, shapes are hoisted to indicate the nature of the vessel.

Fog signals
—— One long blast (4–6 seconds)   • One short blast (2 seconds)

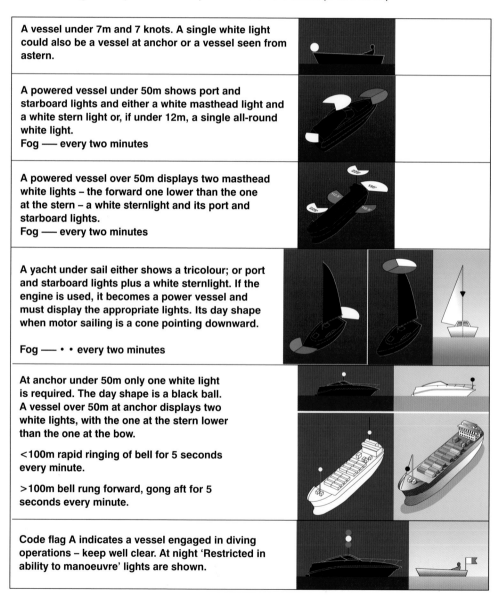

A vessel under 7m and 7 knots. A single white light could also be a vessel at anchor or a vessel seen from astern.	
A powered vessel under 50m shows port and starboard lights and either a white masthead light and a white stern light or, if under 12m, a single all-round white light. Fog —— every two minutes	
A powered vessel over 50m displays two masthead white lights – the forward one lower than the one at the stern – a white sternlight and its port and starboard lights. Fog —— every two minutes	
A yacht under sail either shows a tricolour; or port and starboard lights plus a white sternlight. If the engine is used, it becomes a power vessel and must display the appropriate lights. Its day shape when motor sailing is a cone pointing downward. Fog —— • • every two minutes	
At anchor under 50m only one white light is required. The day shape is a black ball. A vessel over 50m at anchor displays two white lights, with the one at the stern lower than the one at the bow. <100m rapid ringing of bell for 5 seconds every minute. >100m bell rung forward, gong aft for 5 seconds every minute.	
Code flag A indicates a vessel engaged in diving operations – keep well clear. At night 'Restricted in ability to manoeuvre' lights are shown.	

On a sailing yacht under power, its day shape is a cone pointing downward.

Lights, shapes and sounds

A vessel 'not under command', (perhaps a vessel adrift with no means of propulsion) displays two all-round red lights at night or two balls in daylight.

Fog — • • every two minutes

If constrained by draught the vessel displays three all-round vertical red lights or a cylinder during the day.

Fog — • • every two minutes

Vessel 'Restriced in ability to manoeuvre' shows an additional all-round red-white-red combination of lights at night and a ball-diamond-ball during daylight.

Fog — • • every two minutes

Vessel engaged in fishing (but not trawling), displays an additional all-round green light above its all-round white. Two cones apex together by day.

Fog — • • every two minutes

A vessel trawling displays an additional all-round green light above its all-round white. Two cones apex together by day.

Fog — • • every two minutes

A vessel involved in dredging shows 'Restricted in ability to manoeuvre', plus two all-round vertical reds to show which side its gear is out and two all-round vertical greens showing the side that is safe to pass. In daylight, diamonds indicate the safe side and balls indicate the side not to pass.

A vessel towing displays an additional white masthead light if the tow is less than 200m, or two additional white masthead lights if it is greater than 200m. By day diamonds are shown.
Fog — • • every two minutes for both types

UNDER 200m

UNDER 200m

OVER 200m

OVER 200m

A flashing orange light is seen on vessels that travel in non displacement mode – examples include: hovercraft or very fast passenger ferries.

A pilot vessel displays an all-round white over red plus its aspect lights and displays a red and white flag in daylight.

A minesweeper shows three all-round green lights in a triangular pattern at night or three balls in daylight.

Fog —— • • every two minutes

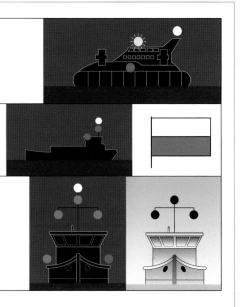

Sound signals

Sounds can be used to indicate what a vessel is about to do. You should have the equipment to make them onboard.

One short blast – I am turning to starboard.

Two short blasts – I am turning to port.

Three short blasts – My engines are going astern – this does not necessarily mean the craft is going backwards.

Five or more short blasts – I don't understand your intentions – perhaps better known as "What on earth are you doing?"

Traffic separation

Traffic separation schemes are denoted on a chart by purple shaded areas. Arrows on the chart denote the direction of the shipping lane. Traffic separation schemes separate large vessels in areas of heavy traffic. Always keep your vessel at right angles to the scheme so that you show the correct aspect to oncoming traffic.

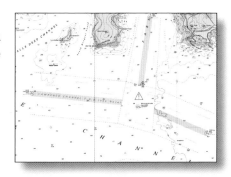

Cruising at speed

Motor boats can cruise at good speeds – some at well over 20 knots, however doing so uses a lot of fuel so you must therefore monitor fuel levels at all times. Cleanliness of the hull will also have a dramatic affect on how much fuel you use.

- The last few revs will use the most fuel so by easing back by about 10% of the rev range you can save over 20% of the fuel!
- Twin engines should be running at the same revs.
- Make sure you tell the crew before making any dramatic changes of throttle to accelerate or decelerate.
- When the boat is fully laden with fuel, passengers or both it will increase the fuel consumption dramatically.
- Always allow a 20% fuel reserve for each passage – this is the minimum contingency for weather or alternative ports.

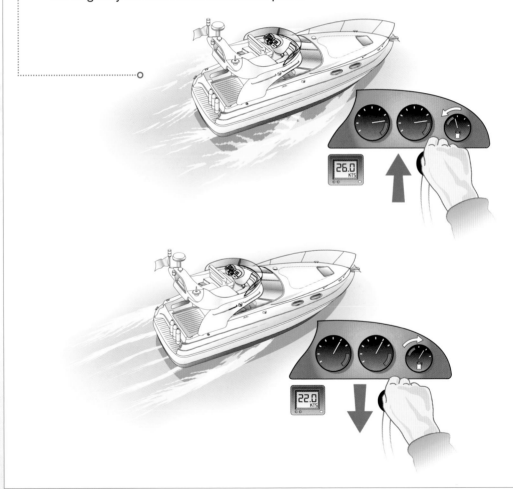

Trim at sea

A boat's trim is expressed in two ways, fore and aft and laterally from side to side. The aim of raising or lowering the bow and stern is to change the boat's attitude and hence its ability to deal with sea conditions for best crew and vessel safety, comfort, fuel consumption and handling characteristics.

Power Trim

Outdrive boats have trim for the outdrive legs, this allows you to change the angle of the propellers' thrust.

For maximum acceleration bring the legs fully in, this helps keep the propellers immersed and gets the boat planing quicker.

Once on the plane, ease the leg out to achieve the best speed, if adjusted correctly the revs will rise slightly without any increase in throttle. This gives best speed and hence fuel consumption for those revs.

If you raise the legs too much the propellers will start to lose grip and suck air down from the surface. The revs will rise but boat speed will drop, the boat may also porpoise. Trim the leg in to regain control.

 Trim needs constant monitoring, crew moving around, changing sea conditions or a decreasing fuel load will all require adjustment.

Trim Tabs

Most larger motor boats have trim tabs which are electrically or mechanically driven plates mounted either side at the stern. They are used either independently or together to alter fore and aft trim or to counter heel from uneven loading or a side wind.

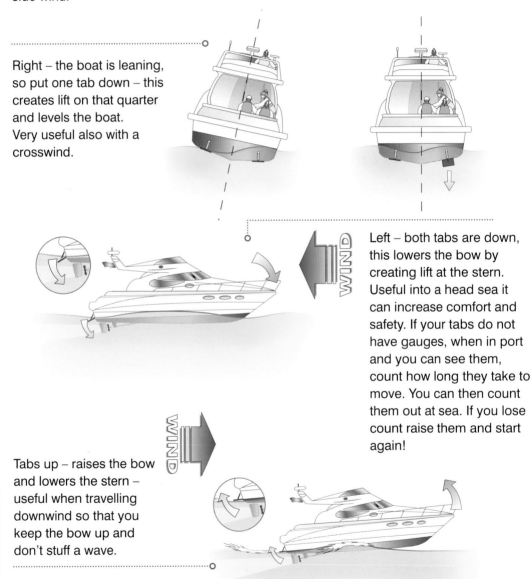

Right – the boat is leaning, so put one tab down – this creates lift on that quarter and levels the boat.
Very useful also with a crosswind.

Left – both tabs are down, this lowers the bow by creating lift at the stern. Useful into a head sea it can increase comfort and safety. If your tabs do not have gauges, when in port and you can see them, count how long they take to move. You can then count them out at sea. If you lose count raise them and start again!

Tabs up – raises the bow and lowers the stern – useful when travelling downwind so that you keep the bow up and don't stuff a wave.

Trim in large waves

Head sea

It's tabs down, so that the slimmer forward vee sections of the hull are doing the work of cutting the waves. This puts most of the boat in the water and reduces slamming.

If tabbed up, the flatter sections of the hull's midsection are taking the slamming and creating lots of spray. This is very tiring!

Outdrives can increase the tabs' effect by trimming in (down) when the tabs are down.

Following sea

It is important to stop the bow burying when the stern is picked up by a wave.

Trim the tabs up so that the bow is up, then adjust your speed to be slower or faster than the waves. For outdrives generally trim the legs to match the tabs.

Cruising at speed

Bigger sea conditions

You really want to go to sea on days when you will enjoy it, but sometimes you may be out in conditions that are more challenging. The sea is very powerful and can do serious damage to a motor boat if it is driven badly in big seas.

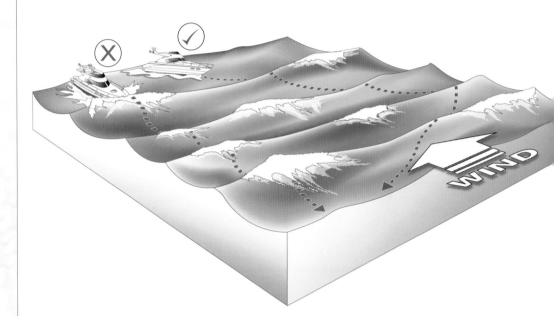

■ Avoid slamming a boat repeatedly into a large head sea.

■ Drive around the waves – it's tiring but makes for a much safer and comfortable passage.

■ You may need to zigzag to make the wave length longer.

■ Reduce your speed to reduce the strain.

■ Consider going to a different port downwind – it may be safer.

■ Downwind is often more comfortable.

Bigger sea dangers

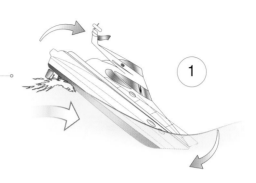

Broaching

This is where a following sea wave crest picks up the stern:

1. This causes the bow to dig in.
2. The boat now slews round to be beam on.
3. You could get rolled over.

To reduce the chance of this happening:

- Adjust your speed downwind to be either faster or slower than the wave crests.
- You may need to tow a drogue to stop the stern being picked up.
- Avoid the breaking crest either on the stern or beam.

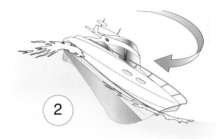

Damage control

Motor boats are at risk of their large window area being broken by the sea. Port holes are usually small to offset this risk. However it is worth carrying blanks (boards) so that you can block off damage. If no blanks, then use bunk cushions or even doors to reduce the water ingress. Again turn downwind towards a port of refuge. Call the Coastguard if you are in danger of sinking.

Man overboard

If you have a man overboard (MOB) situation, then there are some standard actions to take:

1. Shout "Man Overboard" to alert the rest of the crew.
2. Instruct one person to point at the MOB so you do not lose sight.
3. Press the MOB button on the GPS to give a datum and consider throwing a lifebuoy especially if it is rough.
4. Get the boat back upwind of the casualty – and not too close as to endanger them.
5. Use a throw line if it's rough or you are unsure of your close quarter ability.

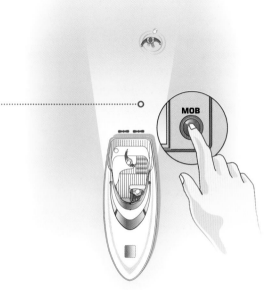

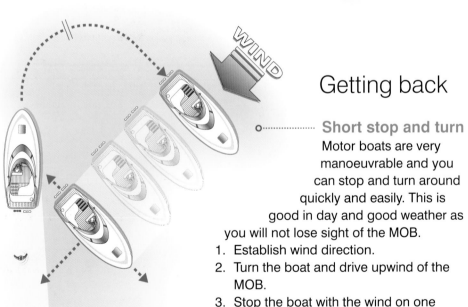

Getting back

Short stop and turn

Motor boats are very manoeuvrable and you can stop and turn around quickly and easily. This is good in day and good weather as you will not lose sight of the MOB.

1. Establish wind direction.
2. Turn the boat and drive upwind of the MOB.
3. Stop the boat with the wind on one beam and the MOB on the other.
4. Drift beam-on down onto the MOB.
5. When close, use only the engine furthest away from the MOB.

The Williamson Turn

Designed to get you back to the MOB whatever the weather, day or night. It is compass orientated and could take you a fair distance from the MOB depending on your turning circle. It developed from large vessels and needs lots of practice to get right.

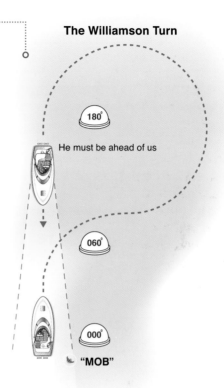

The Williamson Turn

180°

He must be ahead of us

060°

000°

"MOB"

1. Shout of "Man Overboard" goes up, note compass heading check reciprocal.
2. Speed remains constant.
3. Boat steers original course + approx 60° (use full helm).
4. When heading is + 60° reverse helm to hard over the other way.
5. Continue turn until reciprocal of original course is reached.
6. This should bring you back down your original track so slow down.
7. Look for the MOB, and once spotted establish wind direction.
8. Stop upwind as before and drift down onto the MOB.

Casualty recovery

Many motor boats are high sided and even with a bathing platform and ladder, MOB recovery is not easy. You will need to collect the MOB at the area where the side decks are lowest – usually alongside the cockpit and then attach a line and walk them to your recovery area.

When recovered you need to decide if they need any hospitalisation or they may just need:
- Drying off and dry clothes.
- Re-warming slowly. Giving warm (not hot) drinks.
- Use a thermal protection bag (TPA) if no dry clothes available.
- Monitoring consistently at 15 minute intervals.
- If at all unsure call for qualified help!

If you have a situation that presents 'Grave and Imminent Danger to the vessel or persons aboard', then you have a Mayday situation.

There are several ways to alert others to your situation, such as VHF, flares, SOS, flags, EPIRB, foghorn.

Flares

 Brief all crew on where the flares are kept

All flares are fired or held downwind – the angle depends on how windy

Use gloves and goggles

Flares should be in date and kept in a waterproof container

Red Pin Point – best at night if close to help or to alert rescuers of which vessel you are

Orange Smoke – best by day if close to help or to alert rescuers of which vessel you are. Also good for indicating wind direction to a helicopter

Red Parachute – use if not close to help. **Do not fire if a helicopter is present**

If low cloud fire at 45° angle

Other distress signals

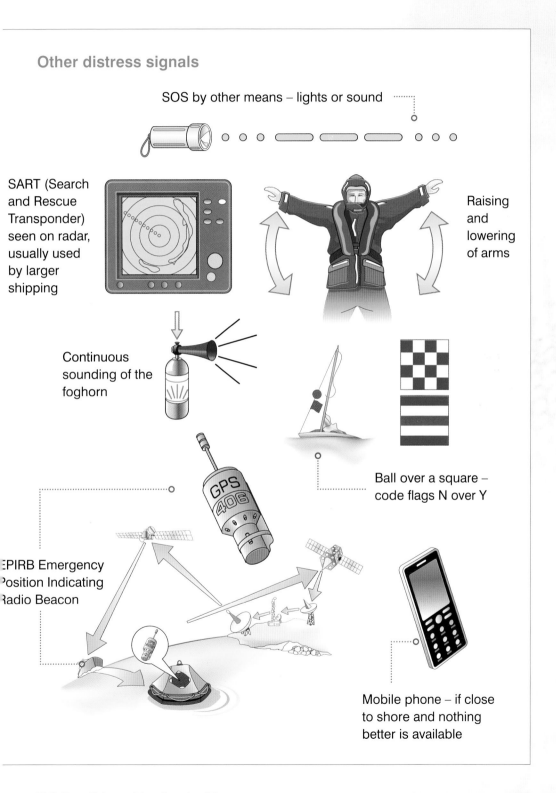

SOS by other means – lights or sound

SART (Search and Rescue Transponder) seen on radar, usually used by larger shipping

Raising and lowering of arms

Continuous sounding of the foghorn

Ball over a square – code flags N over Y

EPIRB Emergency Position Indicating Radio Beacon

Mobile phone – if close to shore and nothing better is available

Emergency situations

VHF Voice call and/or DSC

If you have a VHF DSC radio fitted which is programmed with your MMSI and connected to a GPS you can send a digital distress call. This is very quick and simple:

1. Simply open the cover
2. Press and hold the red button for 5 seconds
3. If time, select what the mayday reason is from the menu (e.g. MOB)

You can also use the normal VHF radio to send a traditional VHF voice message You must tell them:

- Your boat's name
- Your position
- How many people are aboard
- What assistance you require

A VHF radio is better than a mobile phone for a distress situation as other vessels in your area will hear it and could relay it to the Coastguard if you were out of range. The Coastguard can also fix your position from the transmission.

MAYDAY

> **When life or vessel are in Grave or Imminent Danger:**
> Mayday x 3
> This is Motor boat Astrid x 3
> Mayday Motor boat Astrid
> Give MMSI if fitted with DSC
> My position is 50°15'5N 03°31'6W
> We have a person overboard and require immediate assistance
> 3 persons onboard
> Over

PAN PAN

> **Urgency Message – if crew or vessel needs assistance:**
> Pan Pan x 3
> All ships x 3
> This is Motor boat Astrid x 3
> Mayday Motor boat Astrid
> Give MMSI if fitted with DSC
> My position is 50°15'5N 03°31'6W
> We have broken down and require a tow

Even though you need a VHF Operators licence to use the VHF you can use it in a distress call and under the supervision of a person who holds one.

Fire Control

Fires need three things to exist, fuel, air, heat, remove one and it will go out, prevention is much better than cure, so have a fire safe policy.

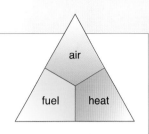

Prevent fires by

No smoking aboard and definitely not below

Be cautious when cooking or cleaning using chemicals

Never use undersize wiring

Keep the engine bay and electrics serviced

Care when using petrol with engines

Fire extinguishers

Should be located by all potential fire points – essential near engine room or galley, and if possible near cabin exits and escape hatches.

If cabins only have one exit route, fit smoke alarms as well as extinguishers.

Have the correct type of extinguishers and carry two fire buckets – they are useful for bailing as well!

Types

■ **Dry Powder** – General purpose, but not for liquids – leaves a mess.

■ **AFFF Foam** – Good on liquids and also for general purposes.

■ **Clean Agent / C02** – Gas for enclosed spaces, good for engine rooms and electrical – no residue.

■ **Fire Blanket** – Excellent for smothering cooking fires, also good in the engine room to cover hot engines while you work on them.

Fire Fighting

The key points are:

Aim at the base of the fire

Smother with a blanket – watch your hands

Splash water rather than chuck it on!

Person on fire – smother clothing preferably with a fire blanket

Engine Fire

Most motor boats have automatic engine room extinguishers. Many can also be operated manually if you suspect a fire. Make sure the crew know how. If you have an engine room fire:

1. Switch off the fuel.
2. Switch off the electrics.
3. If you can, obstruct the air intakes.
4. Do not introduce more air by opening a hatch.
5. If you have extra extinguishers aim them through a fire port.

If the fire is bigger than you can tackle safely:

1. Get ready to abandon ship, put lifejackets on now.
2. Send a Mayday.
3. Launch the liferaft on the upwind side of the boat.

Gas Safety

Gas is a great way to cook afloat, it's quick and efficient, however it is heavier than air and so needs to be treated with respect so accidents do not happen.

- Make sure the crew know how to isolate the gas.
- Keep the gas locker drains clear.
- Get piping and the cooker checked at regular intervals.
- Use the shut off valves.
- Use a gas alarm.

If you have a gas leak
1. Shut off the gas.
2. Shut off the electrics.
3. Open all hatches.
4. Tell all the crew.
5. Ventilate the bilges.
6. Do not smoke.
7. Get the system tested.

Emergency situations

Liferafts

Taking to the liferaft is the absolute last resort – stay with the boat unless it is actually sinking or on fire!

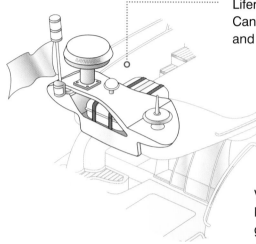

Liferafts come in canisters and valises. Canisters are designed to be fitted outside and are waterproof

Valises are kept in lockers. Don't stow gear on top, you may damage it

Launch the liferaft on the downwind side so the boat does not get blown away from it, the only exception to this is if the boat is on fire.

1. Get the crew into lifejackets.
2. Send a Mayday.
3. Check the painter is tied on.
4. Pull the painter to inflate the raft.
5. Try to get in the raft as dry as possible.
6. Stabilise the raft by putting the heaviest and most able person in the raft first.
7. Always climb into the raft – never jump.
8. Try to take extras – EPIRB, flares, food and drink, extra clothing, TPA's, hand held VHF.
9. When all are in the raft, cut the painter, stream the drogue (to increase stability and reduce drift), close the door to protect from waves and take seasickness tablets, ventilate the raft at least every 30 minutes.

Helicopter Rescue

The helicopter crew will make contact and give a brief of their intentions. If your boat is able to move they will give you a course and speed.

 TIP Follow this information correctly: The crew will lower a weighted line, let it touch the water to earth it and release the static. Do not attach it to the boat, the line is used to guide the winch man – gloves are useful.

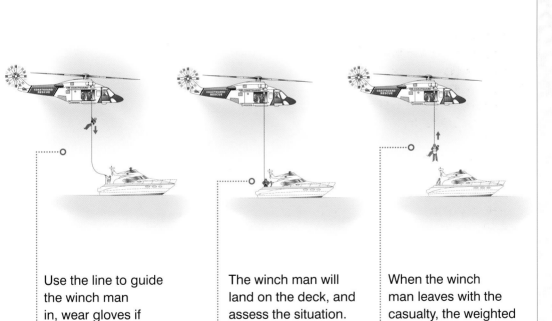

Use the line to guide the winch man in, wear gloves if possible

The winch man will land on the deck, and assess the situation. He is now in control of your boat

When the winch man leaves with the casualty, the weighted line is used to control the ascent

Towing and being towed

Long tow

Towing at sea can create huge loads on both the tug and towed vessel's fittings, so never attempt a tow if the other vessel is much bigger than yours. Even with smaller or similar sized vessels you will still need to spread the load around the boat's strong points using a bridle.

- A long tow is usually only suitable at sea.
- If possible, start the tow by going downwind as it will be easier to pick up momentum before choosing your course.
- Make sure the tug stays clear when passing the line as it could foul your prop.
- You can use a throw line to pass the tow line across.
- Consider a weight on the tow line to reduce snatch.
- The towed vessel may need to stream a drogue to keep it straight.

tug

Short tow

When entering a harbour use an alongside tow for greater manoeuvrability, both vessels need to be well fendered.

- The tug must be further astern than the stern of the towed vessel.
- It helps to toe in the vessels.
- Treat it like a twin engine boat with a single engine.
- It will turn one way better than the other.

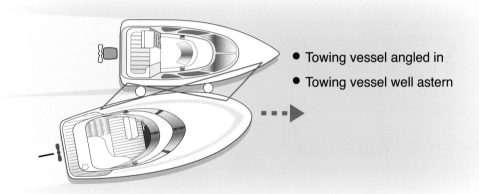

- Towing vessel angled in
- Towing vessel well astern

 TIP   Make an arrangement for any tow fee before you set off, otherwise they could lay a claim to salvage.

Planning a short passage

A short passage is well within the scope of RYA Day Skipper students and the following are the basic steps you need to take into consideration.

- How far is it and how long will it take – do we have sufficient fuel?
- What are the passage constraints – do we need to consider any locks or tidal gates?
- Pilotage – will we arrive or leave in the dark?
- Alternative ports – is there anywhere to stop if we need plan 'B'?
- Weather – do we go? Motor boats are much better in flatter seas.
- Navigation – do we need a course to steer?

Here we have a basic passage based upon RYA Training Chart 3 – this must not be used for navigation!
We want to make a passage from Chidham Marina in Namley Harbour to Dunbarton on the morning of 24th March.

- The distance is approximately 25 miles.
- Boat speed is 10 knots so the passage is about 2½ hours.

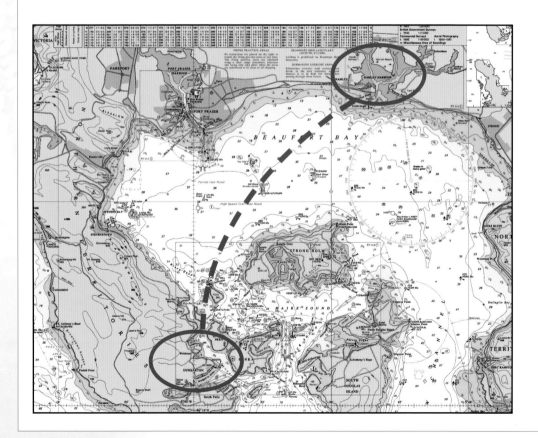

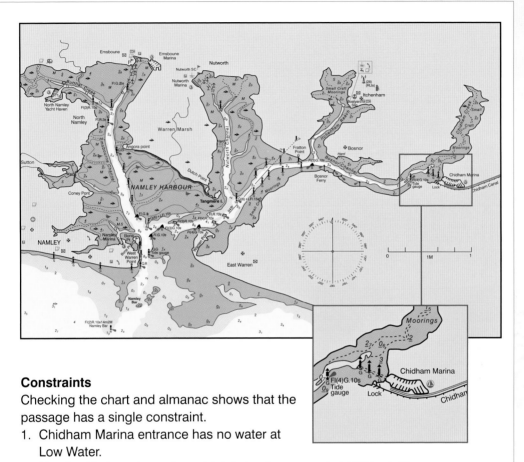

Constraints

Checking the chart and almanac shows that the passage has a single constraint.

1. Chidham Marina entrance has no water at Low Water.
2. Namley Harbour has a bar which is best accessed at H/W +/- 3hours.
3. The almanac shows that Chidham Marina entrance channel is dredged to Chart Datum so we will need a 2m (6ft) rise of tide to give us suitable clearance to leave.

Namley is a Standard Port so we can look at the tide for our chosen day and consult the tidal graph. This indicates that we can leave about 3 hours either side of High Water, as recommended in the almanac.

Therefore our departure is based on HW +/- 3 hours of high water which occurs at 07:05 on the 24th March.

24	0033	1.1
	0705	3.2
SU	1333	1.2
	1945	3.1

Planning a short passage

Estimating time of departure

The weather forecast for the 24th March is North East Force 3 to 4 then veering South East Force 5 to 6 weather fair rain later, this fits well with our plan as we will have a favourable wind with tide scenario for the following hours.

2 hours after HW Victoria

3 hours after HW Victoria

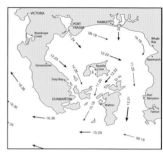

4 hours after HW Victoria

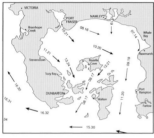

5 hours after HW Victoria

6 hours after HW Victoria

These boxes show the tidal flow based on HW Victoria 06:16 (neaps) on the 24th March. So we have a wind with tide scenario from roughly 07:30 to 11:30.

Our departure window from Chidham Marina ends at 10:05 so combining the two pieces of information would give a nice departure time of 08:00. This allows us 3½ hours of favourable tide to complete a 2½ hour passage.

However by the time we reach the exit to Namley Harbour there would be a cross tide of about 0.9 knots for the first leg of the passage (about 5 miles) so we could consider a course to steer. If it was a Spring Tide with a rate of 1.8 knots then we would almost certainly do a course to steer as this would push us seriously off course.

After the first leg of our passage we will need a pilotage plan to get us through the islands off Dunbarton.

We need to be mindful of the increasing wind strength so have decided to go west of the islands as they will provide more shelter.

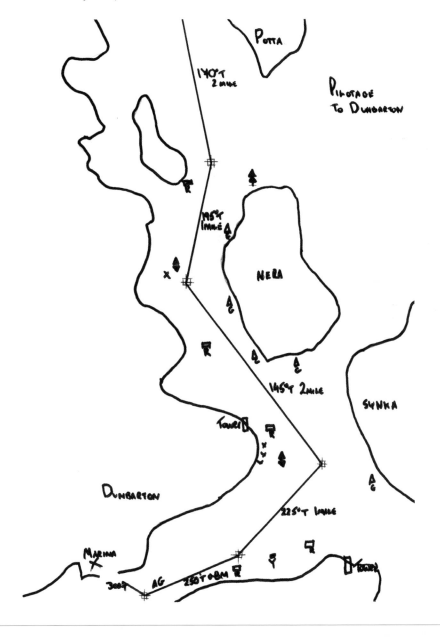

Weather

General view

Weather is dictated by high and low pressure systems that revolve in opposite directions in the two hemispheres. Different areas of the earth's surface have different prevailing patterns that will affect your cruising. The Northern Hemisphere usually has a series of low-pressure systems dictating the weather. In many parts of the Southern Hemisphere a series of cold fronts dictate the weather.

In the Northern Hemisphere low pressure systems revolve anti-clockwise and highs revolve clockwise

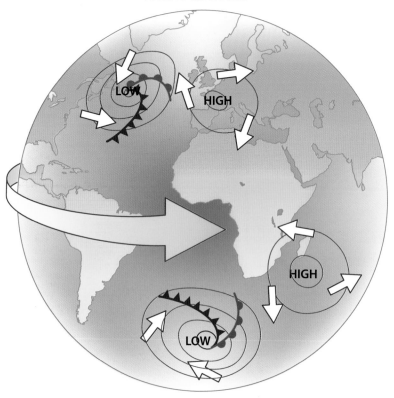

In the Southern Hemisphere low pressure systems revolve clockwise and highs revolve anti-clockwise

High and Low pressure systems

Northern Hemisphere

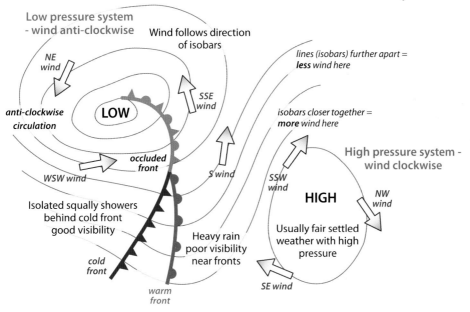

Low pressure system - wind anti-clockwise

Wind follows direction of isobars

NE wind

*lines (isobars) further apart = **less** wind here*

SSE wind

anti-clockwise circulation

LOW

*isobars closer together = **more** wind here*

High pressure system - wind clockwise

occluded front

S wind

SSW wind

NW wind

WSW wind

HIGH

Isolated squally showers behind cold front good visibility

Heavy rain poor visibility near fronts

Usually fair settled weather with high pressure

cold front

warm front

SE wind

Southern Hemisphere

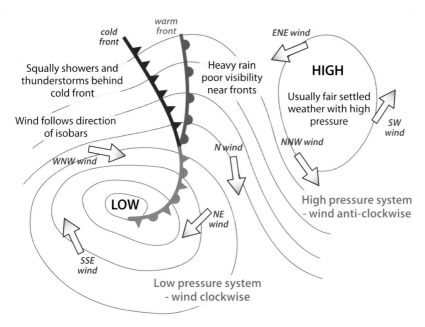

cold front

warm front

ENE wind

HIGH

Squally showers and thunderstorms behind cold front

Heavy rain poor visibility near fronts

Usually fair settled weather with high pressure

SW wind

Wind follows direction of isobars

N wind

NNW wind

WNW wind

High pressure system - wind anti-clockwise

LOW

NE wind

SSE wind

Low pressure system - wind clockwise

Weather

Shipping Forecasts

Listening to the shipping forecast used to be the centre of a boater's decision as to whether to go out. Now the amount of information available via the web means that the radio shipping forecast has often become the last piece in the weather jigsaw puzzle. However once underway and on passage, especially if a longer one, then a radio broadcast of the latest forecast is incredibly useful. It is worth knowing the Shipping Forecast areas and what the terms used mean.

Other useful sources are

- Marine safety information via VHF from the Coastguard.
- Marine weather forecasting via the web or marina office.
- Navtex onboard.

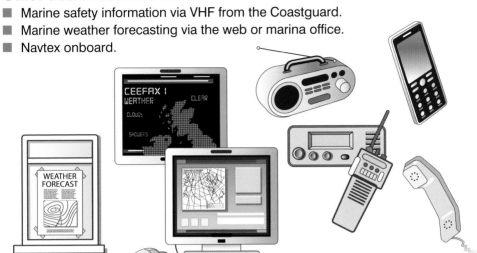

TERMS USED IN FORECASTS	
Gale Warnings	If average wind speed is expected to be F8 or more, or gusts 43 – 51Kn
Strong Wind	If average wind speed is expected to be F6 or F7
Warnings	F6 is often called a 'yachtsman's gale' – remember that!
Imminent	Within 6hrs of time of issue of warning
Soon	Within 6 – 12 hrs of time of issue of warning
Later	More than 12 hrs from time of issue of warning
Visibility	Good – Greater than 5 miles Moderate – Between 2 – 5 miles Poor – 1000m to 2 miles. Fog less than 1000m
Fair	No significant precipitation
Backing	Wind changing in an anti-clockwise direction e.g. SW to SE
Veering	Wind changing in a clockwise direction e.g. SW to NW
General Synopsis	How and where the weather systems are moving
Sea States	Smooth – wave height 0.2 – 0.5m Slight – wave height 0.5 – 1.25m Moderate – wave height 1.25 – 2.5m Rough – wave height 2.5 – 4m Very Rough – wave height 4 – 6m

Weather

Land and Sea Breezes

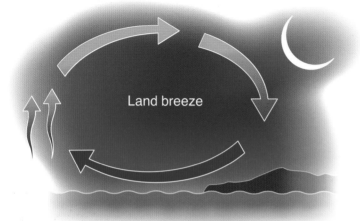

Land Breezes
Can occur on a clear night when the air cools over the land and flows back out to sea, particularly noticeable in river estuaries. Usually a gentle wind no more than Force 2 – 3 unless near mountains.

Sea Breezes
In fair weather and light to moderate offshore winds, a sea breeze is likely to develop. The sun heats the land, the warm air rises and is blown offshore and it then cools, descends and blows onshore. Winds are generally up to Force 4 in strength and up to 25 miles offshore.

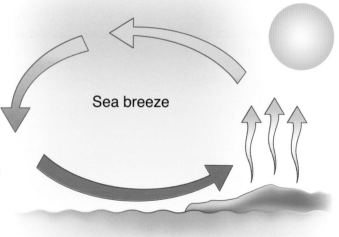

Planning the day

Motor boats are able to make better time and are more comfortable in flatter water. So planning your journey around the weather will make your passage safer and more enjoyable – this is what good skippering is about.

In warm countries you often have a significant sea breeze during the day and passages are more comfortable either side of this period.

Here is the forecast for our earlier planned passage:

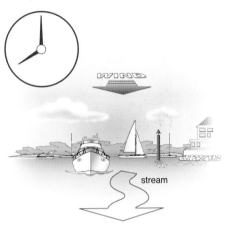

North East Force 3 to 4 then veering South East Force 5 to 6 weather fair rain later.

So if we were to leave early we would have favourable wind and tide for the first period of the passage.

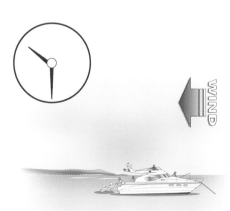

We could even have time to anchor for an early lunch!

Arriving at our destination with freshening wind and tide together. Arrived safely and having had a great day.

Glossary

abeam	to the side of the boat
almanac	book containing tidal information etc on ports
anchor rode	length of rope/chain attached to anchor
backing	wind changing in anti-clockwise direction
beam-on	side-on
Beaufort scale	international scale of wind speed and conditions
blanks	boards carried to replace windows in case of breakage in rough seas
bow thruster	small sideways-mounted prop in bow for manoeuvring
bridle	towing method using single line with two attachment points on vessels
broaching	wave hitting stern of boat, causing it to slew round to be beam on
CE plate	EC requirement on more modern boats stating maximum load
cleat	deck fitting to which mooring lines are attached
displacement craft	slower craft which do not plane on the water
drogue	device towed astern to stabilise boat/liferaft in rough seas
DSC	Digital Selective Calling VHF distress function
EPIRB	Emergency Position Indicating Radio Beacon
fender	shock-absorbing device to protect boat's hull during manoeuvring
fender board	board used with fenders when berthing against uneven wall
ferry gliding	technique for moving sideways across stream
GPS	Global Positioning System
grab bag	bag containing emergency equipment in case of abandoning ship
gunwale	top edge of hull
helm	steering; person who is steering
kedge	type of anchor
lasso	method of temporarily attaching mooring line to buoy
lazy lines	line attached to permanent mooring line on harbour bed
Mayday	message sent when life or vessel are in Grave or Imminent Danger
MMSI	Maritime Mobile Service Identity digital VHF signal
offset turning	turning effect on twin screw boats
outdrives	propulsion system which incorporates steering function
painter	line attached to bow of dinghy/liferaft
Pan Pan	urgency message if crew or vessel needs assistance
pilotage plan	summary of route of passage to be undertaken

pivot points	theoretical point in the boat about which it pivots
planing craft	faster craft which can rise and skim across the water surface
port tack	sailing to windward with wind over port side
propeller pitch	theoretical distance craft will travel on one rotation of propeller
propwash	propeller-generated water flow over the rudder
rafting up	berthing with one or more craft alongside
reciprocal course	course in opposite direction to original
scope	length of rope/chain attached to anchor relative to depth
sea cocks	valves in hull to allow water out (and in)
slamming	action of hull hitting surface of water in rough seas
slip lines	mooring lines which can be detached whilst aboard
snubbing anchor	moving boat forward to allow anchor to dig into seabed
springs	mooring lines run diagonally from boat to berth
stand off vessel	vessel which has to give way
stand on vessel	vessel having right of way
starboard tack	sailing to windward with wind over starboard side
steerage	movement relative to stream that is necessary to allow effective steering
stemming	stopping sideways movement of boat when ferry gliding
stream	movement of water caused by tide or river flow
tacking	sailing in windward direction on zig-zag course
TPA	thermal protection bag
transit	lining up two fixed objects to establish position or movement
tricolour	masthead light showing three colours in three directions
trim	changing the boat's attitude for best safety, comfort, fuel consumption and handling
trim tabs	electrically or mechanically driven plates mounted on either side of stern to adjust trim
tripping line	line used to retrieve anchor if stuck
veering	wind changing in clockwise direction
VHF	Very High Frequency radio
Williamson Turn	method of turning to return on reciprocal course (opposite direction to original)
windage	wind resistance of side area of boat
windlass	winch

Index

RYA Membership

Promoting and Protecting Boating

www.rya.org.uk

RYA Membership

The RYA is the national organisation which represents the interests of everyone who goes boating for pleasure. The greater the membership, the louder our voice when it comes to protecting members' interests. Apply for membership today, and support the RYA, to help the RYA support you.

BENEFITS OF MEMBERSHIP

- Special members' discounts on a range of products and services including boat insurance, books, charts, DVD's and class certificates

- Access to expert advice on all aspects of boating from legal wrangles to training matters

- Free issue of Certificates of Competence, increasingly asked for by everyone from overseas governments to holiday companies, insurance underwriters to boat hirers

- Access to the wide range of RYA publications,including the quarterly magazine

- Third Party insurance for windsurfing members

- Free Internet access with RYA-Online

- Special discounts on AA membership

- Regular offers in RYA Magazine

- ...and much more

JOIN NOW

Membership form opposite or join online at www.rya.org.uk

Visit our website for information, advice, members' services and web shop.

IT'S ALL ABOUT YOU
AND THE BOATING YOU DO

RYA MEMBERSHIP APPLICATION

Be part of it

One of boating's biggest attractions is its freedom from rules and regulations. As an RYA member you'll play an active part in keeping it that way, as well as benefiting from free expert advice and information, plus discounts on a wide range of boating products, charts and publications.

To join the RYA, please complete the application form below and send it to The Membership Department, RYA, RYA House, Ensign Way, Hamble, Southampton, Hampshire SO31 4YA. You can also join online at www.rya.org.uk, or by phoning the membership department on +44 (0) 23 8060 4159. Whichever way you choose to apply, you can save money by paying by Direct Debit. A Direct Debit instruction is on the back of this form.

	Title	Forename	Surname	Gender	Date of Birth
Applicant ❶					/ /
Applicant ❷					/ /
Applicant ❸					/ /
Applicant ❹					/ /

Address

Post Code

Home Tel

Day Time Tel

Mobile Tel

E-mail Applicant ❶

E-mail Applicant ❷

E-mail Applicant ❸

E-mail Applicant ❹

Type of membership required (Tick Box)

Junior (0-11) Annual rate £5 or **£5 if paying by Direct Debit**
Youth (12-17) Annual rate £14 or **£11 if paying by Direct Debit**
Under 25 Annual rate £25 or **£22 if paying by Direct Debit**
Personal Annual rate £43 or **£39 if paying by Direct Debit**
Family* Annual rate £63 or **£59 if paying by Direct Debit**

Please number up to three boating interests in order, with number one being your principal interest

Yacht Racing	Yacht Cruising	Dinghy Racing	Dinghy Cruising
Personal Watercraft	Sportboats & RIBs	Windsurfing	Motor Boating
Powerboat Racing	Canal Cruising	River Cruising	

* *Family Membership: 2 adults plus any under 18s all living at the same address. Prices valid until 30/9/2011 One discount voucher is accepted for individual memberships, and two discount vouchers are accepted for family membership.*

Save money by completing the Direct Debit form overleaf

IMPORTANT In order to provide you with membership benefits the details provided by you on this form and in the course of your membership will be maintained on a database. If you do not wish to receive information on member services and benefits please tick here ☐ By applying for membership of the RYA you agree to be bound by the RYA's standard terms and conditions (copies on request or at www.rya.org.uk)

Signature

Date / /

Source Code

Joining Point Code

GET MORE FROM
YOUR
BOATING
SUPPORT THE
RYA

Instructions to your Bank or Building Society to pay by Direct Debit

Please fill in the form and send to:

Membership Department, Royal Yachting Association, RYA House, Ensign Way, Hamble,
Southampton, Hampshire SO31 4YA.

Be part of it

Name and full postal address of your Bank/Building Society

To the Manager | Bank/Building Society

Address

Postcode

Name(s) of Account Holder(s)

Branch Sort Code

☐☐ – ☐☐ – ☐☐

Bank/Building Society Account Number

☐☐☐☐☐☐☐☐

Originator's Identification Number

| 9 | 5 | 5 | 2 | 1 | 3 |

RYA Membership Number (For office use only)

☐☐☐☐☐☐☐

Instructions to your Bank or Building Society

Please pay Royal Yachting Association Direct Debits from the account detailed in
this instruction subject to the safeguards assured by The Direct Debit Guarantee.
I understand that this instruction may remain with the Royal Yachting Association
and, if so, details will be passed electronically to my Bank/Building Society.

Signature(s)

Date: D D / M M / Y Y Y Y